Happy B
Vince

love Mom & Dad

Wise

2007

THROUGH WATER, ICE & FIRE

The Lord continue
to bless you in
all you do.

Other books by Barry Gough

The Royal Navy and the Northwest Coast of North America, 1810–1914

Canada

To the Pacific and Arctic with Beechey: The Journal of Lieutenant George Peard of H.M.S. Blossom, 1825–1828

The Northwest Coast: British Navigation, Trade, and Discoveries to 1812 (first edition published as *Distant Dominion: Britain and the Northwest Coast of North America, 1579–1809*)

Gunboat Frontier: British Maritime Authority and Northwest Coast Indians, 1846–1890

The Journal of Alexander Henry the Younger, 1799–1814

British Mercantile Interests in the Making of the Peace of Paris, 1763: War, Trade and Empire

First across the Continent: Sir Alexander Mackenzie

Historical Dictionary of Canada

H.M.C.S. Haida: *Battle Ensign Flying*

Fighting Sail on Lake Huron and Georgian Bay: The War of 1812 and Its Aftermath

Britain, Canada and the North Pacific: Maritime Enterprise and Dominion, 1778–1914

Barry Gough

THROUGH WATER, ICE & FIRE

Schooner *Nancy* of the War of 1812

THE DUNDURN GROUP
TORONTO

Copy-Editor: Lloyd Davis
Design: Andrew Roberts
Printer: Marquis

Library and Archives Canada Cataloguing in Publication

Gough, Barry M., 1938-

    Through water, ice & fire : Schooner Nancy of the War of 1812 / Barry Gough.

Includes bibliographical references.

ISBN-10: 1-55002-569-4
ISBN-13: 978-1-55002-569-9

    1. Nancy (Ship).   2. Canada--History--War of 1812--Naval operations.

I. Title.

FC449.N3G68 2006   971.03'4   C2005-906319-X

1   2   3   4   5   10   09   08   07   06

Conseil des Arts du Canada   Canada Council for the Arts   Canada   ONTARIO ARTS COUNCIL CONSEIL DES ARTS DE L'ONTARIO

We acknowledge the support of the Canada Council for the Arts and the Ontario Arts Council for our publishing program. We also acknowledge the financial support of the Government of Canada through the Book Publishing Industry Development Program and The Association for the Export of Canadian Books, and the Government of Ontario through the Ontario Book Publishers Tax Credit program, and the Ontario Media Development Corporation.

Care has been taken to trace the ownership of copyright material used in this book. The author and the publisher welcome any information enabling them to rectify any references or credits in subsequent editions.

J. Kirk Howard, President

Printed and bound in Canada.
Printed on recycled paper.

www.dundurn.com

Dundurn Press	Gazelle Book Services Limited	Dundurn Press
3 Church Street, Suite 500	White Cross Mills	2250 Military Road
Toronto, Ontario, Canada	High Town, Lancaster, England	Tonawanda, NY
M5E 1M2	LA1 4XS	U.S.A. 14150

THROUGH WATER, ICE & FIRE

To the memory of Stan Rogers, balladeer of the heroic Nancy, and keeper of the flame of Canada's sea history

Contents

Acknowledgements

$\mathcal{I}$t is a pleasure to thank the following repositories and institutions for historical materials used in this book: Parks Ontario (Wasaga Beach Provincial Park); Penetanguishene Public Library; the Archives of Ontario; Parks Canada; the National Archives of Canada; the Marine Museum of the Great Lakes in Kingston, Ontario; the Marine Museum of Upper Canada in Toronto; Hamilton Public Library; the Library of the Royal Military College of Canada; the Royal Canadian Military Institute Library; Naval Historical Center of the United States Department of the Navy; Special Collections of the University of California San Diego Libraries; The Boston Athenaeum; Rhode Island Historical Society; the National Archives; the National Maritime Museum; and the Department of Manuscripts, British Library. In particular I thank Maurice Smith, William S. Dudley, Michael Crawford, Kenneth Hagan, Spencer Tucker, Reginald Horsman, David Skaggs, Graeme Mount, Grant Head, James Seay Dean, Rych Mills, Harold Russell, Keith Widder, Chris Anderson, John Gibson, A.J. McLaughlin, Lynda Claassen, Peter Rindlisbacher, James Barry and Suzanne Stark.

In researching the further particulars on which this book is based, I thank Christopher Arajs of Queen's University and Wilfrid Laurier University. David Arajs assisted with illustrations. As with my previous writings on the War of 1812, this book owes much to the senior seminar in History at Wilfrid Laurier University that put period documents under the microscope, so to speak, with surprising new yields. This document collection will be found among my archives at Wilfrid Laurier University.

Every effort has been made to communicate with holders of copyright in original materials. Documentation and material quoted comes by permission of the Archives of Ontario, the National Archives of Canada and the United States National Archives. I acknowledge the permission of the Controller of Her Majesty's Stationery Office to quote unpublished Crown Copyright material in the National Archives. I am grateful to Peter Rindlisbacher for permission to use his fine illustrations. To many others who have supplied information or advice, I extend my thanks. I alone am responsible for errors or omissions in this work.

Barry Gough
Victoria, British Columbia

Preface

This story of the famous Great Lakes schooner *Nancy* has been a labour of love both in the research and the telling. Few such vessels have captured the imagination of students of Canadian history. Among the treasured vessels of our past, the *Nancy* ranks alongside Cabot's *Mathew*, Cartier's *Hermione*, LaSalle's *Griffon*, the HBC's *Beaver* and Larsen's *St. Roch*. The *Nancy*'s story is particularly fabled because of her cross-border escapades during the War of 1812, when her risky voyages to the southwest shore of Lake Erie helped sustain the British Imperial campaign at Sandusky and the River Raisin, one of the most vicious fights of the conflict. Then, too, her fiery end, in battle against vessels of the United States Navy in 1814 on the Nottawasaga River, marks another important chapter in that remarkable struggle for control of the inland seas.

In recounting the legendary voyages of the *Nancy* and her epic final hours I have also sought to tell the story of her two great masters, Alexander Mackintosh and Miller Worsley. The former was a merchant captain; the latter, a British naval officer. Both of them fought patriotically for the British Imperial side and were, in their separate ways, models of the zeal, determination and heroic character that were exhibited in these enchanting but ruthless days of fighting sail. Their names live on, albeit somewhat in the shadow of *Nancy*'s illustrious glory. But we must remember that ships are instruments of commerce or war, and historical credit is due to those who sail them and provide leadership, technical knowledge, and the ability to command. Also, serving under their command were skilled men. The crews that worked the *Nancy* deserve greater credit than the historical record gives them. However, as is the case with so many other gallant figures, the records of their story have been lost to time. What little remains of our knowledge of these men has been carefully preserved in these pages. With this in mind, I have taken care to tell more about Mackintosh and Worsley than previous accounts have given. They are, in a way, heroes of the piece: figures against a horizon, then engulfed in the flames of combat. It is a world we have lost, but almost two hundred years later it has a romance and a wonder that calls out for the telling.

This book extends the *Nancy* story as analyzed in *Fighting Sail on Lake Huron and Georgian Bay: The War of 1812 and Its Aftermath* (Naval Institute Press and Vanwell Publishing, 2002). It examines details and aspects of this freshwater war that have not previously been looked at. That war, as told through a ship's life, has its own charm as well as its own dynamic. In latter years, as official historian of Canada's most treasured man-of-war, HMCS *Haida*, I have learned (even more so than in my days as a sailor and serviceman) that the material of war — in this case a Tribal-class destroyer, now a Parks Canada and Canadian Historical Site in Hamilton, Ontario — becomes the symbol for those who used such a weapons platform in wartime. The same is true of the *Nancy*. The era is different, of course, but the same principle applies. We still have the charred bones of the *Nancy*, saved for posterity by my zealous precursor, the journalist C.J.H. Snider, at the museum at Wasaga Beach, Ontario. These ships cry out their stories to us from across the generations. They are a reminder, as I say, of a world now lost; even so, they are an enchanting monument to past ages of maritime endeavour and the Price of Admiralty.

No account of the trial and tragic end of the *Nancy* would be complete without the story of how Worsley avenged the loss of the schooner. That chapter is a saga of derring-do and cunning the likes of which were characteristic of its time, and it has not lost anything in the retelling. For with Worsley's capture of the U.S. Navy's *Tigress* and *Scorpion*, the tide of the war on Lake Huron turned — boosting the fortunes of the Royal Navy, various army units, the North West Company, and Indian allies considerably. What would have happened had another year's campaigning occurred is not difficult to guess. But just as fortune had favoured the brave, so did urgent diplomacy bring peace to the lakeland frontier and borderlands, so that Worsley's prizes remained British naval property and central to British strategy on the Great Lakes in the immediate post-war period, the last years of fighting sail.

Timeline

24 November 1789	The *Nancy* is launched
1805	Alexander Mackintosh takes command of the *Nancy*
18 June 1812	The United States declares war on Great Britain
1 July 1812	The *Nancy* is moved to Fort Malden for protection
12 July 1812	Brigadier General William Hull invades Canada
17 July 1812	Michilimackinac is captured
30 July 1812	The *Nancy* transports reinforcements to Amherstburg
16 August 1812	Brock captures Detroit
17 August 1812	The *Nancy* begins transporting American prisoners of war
8 October 1812	Lieutenant Jesse Elliot, USN, captures the *Caledonia*
13 October 1812	The Battle of Queenston Heights
Winter 1812–13	The *Nancy* winters at Moy
22 January 1813	The Battle of Frenchtown
23 April 1813	The *Nancy* and other vessels transport the British army for its attack on Fort Meigs
27 April 1813	York is captured by U.S. forces
14 May 1813	After the siege of Fort Meigs fails, *Nancy* returns to Moy
19 June 1813	Boats from Black Rock arrive at Erie
19 July 1813	The *Nancy* and other vessels transport troops for a second attack on Fort Meigs

28 July 1813	The *Nancy* and other vessels transport troops to Fort Stephenson
2 August 1813	After the British attack on Fort Stephenson fails, *Nancy* returns to Moy
31 August 1813	The *Nancy* sails for Michilimackinac
10 September 1813	The Battle of Put-in-Bay
4 October 1813	The *Nancy* arrives at the St. Clair River
5 October 1813	The Battle of Moraviantown
6 October 1813	The *Nancy* fights on the St. Clair River
19 October 1813	The *Nancy* arrives at Michilimackinac
28 October 1813	Canoes are sent from Michilimackinac to Matchedash Bay for supplies
Winter 1813–14	The *Nancy* winters at Sault Ste. Marie
29 April 1814	Arthur Sinclair takes command of the U.S.'s Lake Erie squadron
Spring 1814	The *Nancy* carries supplies to Michilimackinac
14 May 1814	Port Dover is burned
2 August 1814	Lieutenant Miller Worsley, RN, takes command of the *Nancy*
4 August 1814	The American attack on Michilimackinac fails
14 August 1814	The *Nancy* is destroyed in the Nottawasaga River
3 September 1814	The *Tigress* is captured
6 September 1814	The *Scorpion* is captured
24 December 1814	The Treaty of Ghent ends the War of 1812
August 1911	C.H.J. Snider finds the *Nancy*'s remains
July 1927	Dr. F.J. Conboy excavates the *Nancy*'s remains

Introduction

The War of 1812 occupies a special place in the histories of both Canada and the United States. It was in many respects the beginning of national consolidation on both sides. Both Canadians and Americans exited the war with a fresh and fertile ground on which to sow their national identities. The war also allowed Great Britain and the United States to settle their formal boundaries west of the Continental Divide. This gives the War of 1812 the honour of not only being the war that defined two nations psychologically, but physically as well. Despite this remarkable place in the history of North America, the War of 1812 is all but forgotten. In recent years, only a handful of historians in either Canada or the United States have dabbled in it, and even fewer have made it their specialty. In Great Britain, the war goes largely unnoticed.

The story of the *Nancy*, like the War of 1812 itself, is vital and yet forgotten. Following the War of 1812 the story of the schooner was largely lost, or simply retold superficially as parts of larger histories. It was not until the twentieth century, when Colonel E.A. Cruikshank published a short article in the *Ontario Historical Review*, that a more complete story was brought to light. C.H.J. Snider, a journalist from Toronto, crafted the fullest history of the *Nancy* in 1913 with *In the Wake of the Eighteen-Twelvers*. Snider later published *Leaves from the War Log of the* Nancy, a transcription of the few months of the *Nancy*'s log that have survived history. Not until the publication of my *Fighting Sail on Lake Huron and Georgian Bay: The War of 1812 and Its*

Aftermath was the *Nancy* placed in its historical context. What remains now is to tell the story as it ought to be told, as an adventure of the *Nancy* and her gallant little band of seamen amid the broader dangers of the War of 1812.

The *Nancy*'s war took place on one of the most strategic battle-grounds of the War of 1812. The Northwest, or "Old Northwest" as American textbooks term it, was defined as that area comprising what is now western and northern Ontario, Michigan, Wisconsin, Illinois, Indiana and Ohio. From the outset of the War of 1812 the Northwest was a crucial battleground. Economically vital to the British, politically indispensable to the Americans, and the homeland of dozens of Native nations, the Northwest became a campaign ground that taxed the resources, manpower and strategic thought of all sides of the conflict. The war for the Northwest, however, was not simply a set-piece battle-field where soldiers marched and died like men on a chessboard. It was, above all else, a supply war. It was a war where disease and weather could cripple an army and where food was scarce and communications slow. It was a war where little schooners like the *Nancy* represented the difference between victory and defeat.

To tell the story of the *Nancy*, it is essential that the story of the war in the Northwest be told. That being said, this is not meant to be a campaign history. Events will move quickly and the emphasis will return to the little schooner as often as history allows. It should be borne in mind, however, that everything the *Nancy* encountered was impacted by the wider world around her.

The Old Northwest

On 1 July 1812, Alexander Mackintosh looked with pride on his little schooner, for she was designed and built for speed, maneuverability, and durability — perfect for Great Lakes waters. *Nancy* lay quietly at the Mackintosh family wharf at this western rim of the Upper Canada peninsula, hard by the waterway that separated British from American territory. Her sails were neatly furled and tucked under her yardarms. She was a handsome, if somewhat aging, vessel. At twenty-five years of age, Alexander was only two years older than his schooner. The *Nancy* had been built across the river in Detroit by Forsyth, Richardson & Co., date of completion 24 December 1789. Her two raked masts were rigged both for square topsails and fore-and-aft mainsails. She measured eighty feet long and twenty-two feet wide, and was made of the sturdiest white oak and cedar. A graceful figurehead of a fashionably dressed lady, complete with a hat and feather, pointed the way at *Nancy*'s bow. While her exterior was sturdy, if a little worn, inside Mackintosh's cabin was spacious and comfortable, with large stern windows allowing a flood of light. More importantly, her hold was a cavernous eight feet deep, capable of carrying 350 barrels of cargo.[1] For the kind of protection the uncertain and sometimes dangerous fur trade demanded, Mackintosh had two small brass cannon mounted on her deck.

The *Nancy* was part of a vast fur-trading network managed by Angus Mackintosh, Alexander's father. Angus was one of the powerful

Forsyth, Richardson and Company built the schooner *Nancy* at Detroit in 1789. She served as a civilian transport on the Great Lakes until the War of 1812, when she entered the employ of the British forces. In 1814 the Royal Navy assumed control of the little schooner and renamed her HM Schooner *Nancy*. She supplied the British garrison at Michilimackinac with vital provisions during summer, 1814. American forces, under Commodore Arthur Sinclair, destroyed the *Nancy* on 14 August 1814. (From *HMS Nancy and the War of 1812*, 1978)

North West Company's agents in the Detroit area.[2] Born in 1755 into the family of McIntosh clan chieftainship, Angus had left Scotland in his youth. By 1783 he had settled near Detroit and married into a local French family. There, his business and his family prospered. When Detroit was passed to the Americans by the 1783 treaty, Angus moved his family to the British side of the river, where he built a large two-storey house, a warehouse, a wharf and a store where he could sell the goods he shipped around the lakes. He called the complex Moy, after his family's ancestral home in Scotland. He and his wife had fourteen children — including ten daughters and four sons. Alexander was the second-oldest.[3]

To help maintain the efficiency of their lake shipping route, Angus and the North West Company bought the *Nancy* shortly before the turn of the century. The transportation business was so successful that Angus built another fur-trade schooner, the *Caledonia*, at Moy in 1799, and became part owner of another vessel, the *Charlotte*. Together with the *Nancy*, these ships ferried goods from all points on lakes Erie and Huron and formed a vital link in the North West Company's trading network. They shipped sugar, food and other products to the northern fur trade posts of St. Joseph's Island, Michilimackinac and Sault Ste. Marie. On the return voyages, their holds were filled with valuable packs of fur. When the opportunity permitted, Angus contracted out his vessels to other fur-trading merchants.[4]

The Mackintoshes were respected and well-liked members of the community. Angus's ships regularly carried out small personal favours for the friends of the Mackintosh family. Alexander would deliver letters, packages or cargo back and forth between John Askin Sr. at Amherstburg, and his son John Jr., who was living on St. Joseph's Island, as favours. As a representative of the North West Company, Angus and Alexander had to be careful not to help their competitors too much. But for their friends and neighbours, generous allowances were made. As John Askin Sr. wrote glowingly to one of his children, "I think Mr. Mackintosh disposed to oblige any of the family, when he can do it without drawing blame on himself from the NWC."[5]

Alexander had assumed command of his father's *Nancy* in 1805. Though barely eighteen years of age, the responsibility of the schooner

A topmast schooner, the *Nancy* had two fore-and-aft rigged masts each topped with square sails. Although the rig was arguably outdated by the time of the War of 1812, the *Nancy* nevertheless proved to be a good sailer until her destruction in 1814. This model, built in the 1920s, is housed in the Museum of the Upper Lakes, Wasaga Beach, Ontario. (From *The Museum of the Upper Lakes, Wasaga Beach Ontario*, no date)

rested well with Alexander Mackintosh, and he flourished as its commander for years. Alexander, of self-assured and fiery disposition, had a
good deal of Scottish thistle in him. He was, as events proved, a glorious
and defiant scrapper. He was proud of his swift, nimble vessel. Eight
other men helped Alexander sail the *Nancy*. Jacob Hammond was first
mate, and second-in-command. Evan Richards was the cook. Jonas
Butler Parker was the carpenter, and Joseph Lamotte, carpenter's mate.
Richard McGregor, John Morrison, Joseph Paquet and John Baptiste
Tromp were all seamen. This ship's company navigated the *Nancy*
through the wooded shores of the upper Great Lakes, and in 1812 they
navigated her through the coming storm of war with the United States.

Knit snugly against the banks of the Detroit River, Sandwich and
Moy, now the automotive city of Windsor, were directly opposite the
fortified American town of Detroit. For nearly twenty years, residents
on both sides of the river had existed in relative peace and tranquility.
The Detroit River and its northerly counterpart the St. Clair were the
great highways to the fur lands north and west of the Great Lakes. The
gateway to these lands stood at Michilimackinac, a small island in the
straits connecting Lake Huron with Lake Michigan. To the east lay the
main artery of trade, through Lake Erie, along the banks of the Niagara
River, and then down Lake Ontario to the St. Lawrence, the Atlantic, and
the wider world.

Buried at the very end of these trading lines, the merchants of the
Detroit River made their living delivering goods back and forth
between the Northwest and the eastern fur markets of Montreal, New
York and Europe. Ferrying goods between Michilimackinac — or
Mackinac as it was sometimes called — and the eastern end of Lake
Erie required a special sort of small schooner, one that had a draft
shallow enough to transit the rapids of the St. Clair, but which also had
a hold deep enough to accommodate sufficient fur goods to make the
trip profitable.

The *Nancy* was such a vessel. The spring after her launch in 1789,
she had sailed from Detroit to Fort Erie, on the Canadian side of the
Niagara River. There she filled her hold with cargo and sailed up Lake
Huron to Sault Ste. Marie.[6] For the next twenty-three years the *Nancy*
made similar runs to the various trading depots along the upper Great

The charming figurehead "of a lady dressed in the present fashion with a hat and feather," adorned *Nancy*'s bow, carved by Skelling, of New York, was a bright source of pride to builders and owners of the schooner. This recreation hangs in the Museum of the Upper Lakes, Wasaga Beach, Ontario. (From *HMS Nancy and the War of 1812*, 1978)

Lakes, and she and others like her maintained the growing fur trade to the northwest.

A loosely knit organization of merchants, the Montreal-based North West Company, dominated that fur trade. It operated in the middle ground between the territories of the Hudson's Bay Company to the north, and the American Fur Company to the south. Using Fort William, at the extreme western edge of Lake Superior, as their rendezvous and depot, the North West Company's men aggressively pushed their trade through the creeks, rivers and little lakes to the west and north of the Great Lakes. They brought trade goods from Montreal and sent their agents ever farther westward, to and beyond the Rocky Mountains, in search of more and better pelts for export to the European market. That trade expanded quickly: by 1811, Canadian traders were doing business west of the Continental Divide, and the explorer David Thompson had arrived at the mouth of the Columbia River.

The aggressiveness and efficiency of the North West Company made it a successful competitor. The Hudson's Bay Company, operating from posts on Hudson Bay and inland along river tributaries, found itself cut off at the source from the best pelts. Similarly, the American Fur Company found itself battling for Native partners in the upper reaches of the Mississippi and in the areas that are now Michigan and Wisconsin. By 1812 the lucrative fur trade, long the lifeblood of Quebec, had become the backbone of the Upper Canadian economy, and the key to controlling the interior of the continent.

For generations, the fur traders had conducted business with the Native tribes of the North American interior. The fur trade was as integral to the economies of the various Native groups as it was to the European colonists. Manufactured goods, weapons, ammunition and information all passed in and out of the Northwest and the Great Lakes via the fur-trading network. Those who hoped to control this network had to maintain good relations with colonial and Native leaders alike; they also had to hold sway over water access to the Northwest.

In 1812 the North West Company controlled the network, and did so very efficiently through three main routes. The first was the Ottawa and French River route. The North West Company could bring their trade goods north and west from Montreal up the Ottawa River, then

Lake Huron, the lake that links the others, was a strategic body of water in the early nineteenth century. Much of Angus Mackintosh's business came from transporting goods for the lucrative fur trade via Lake Erie to the various posts on the Upper Great Lakes. During the War of 1812 American and British forces necessarily fought for control of the lake. The result was the British capture of Michilimackinac, the American burning of Sault Ste. Marie, the destruction of the *Nancy*, and Lieutenant Miller Worsely's avenging capture of the *Tigress* and the *Scorpion*. ("Chart of Lake Huron" by Henry W. Howlett Bayfield / Library and Archives Canada / NMC 21705)

down the French River into Georgian Bay. From there they could send their canoes to present-day Sault Ste. Marie, up into Lake Superior and through Fort William to the lakes and rivers of the Red River Valley and even farther west. Alternatively, the canoes could go directly west to Michilimackinac, the gateway to the fur trade in the vicinity of Lake Michigan and the upper Mississippi River. From this tiny island outpost, fur traders could carry their goods deep into the North American interior to such places as Chicago, Milwaukee, Green Bay and Prairie du Chien. There, various Native nations with a long history of good business relations with the North West Company could bring their furs and exchange them for manufactured goods, tobacco, liquor, foodstuffs and weapons.

The second route extended from Montreal, down through Lake Ontario to the town of Newark (now Niagara-on-the-Lake) at the entrance of the Niagara River. At Newark, goods and people could be loaded onto riverboats that took them to Queenstown (Queenston), where a short overland portage brought them around the imposing Niagara Falls and to the small town of Chippawa. From Chippawa, the goods could be loaded back onto boats and taken to the supply depot at Fort Erie, a small British military bastion at the southern end of the Niagara River. From Fort Erie, schooners could take the goods up Lake Erie to Detroit on the St. Clair River and then north, to Grand Portage, Michilimakinac, or even Lake Michigan.

The third was a relatively new and little used overland route. From Montreal, goods could be taken once again to Lake Ontario; at York — modern-day Toronto — they could be taken north along a roughly hacked trail, which is now Yonge Street. The trail took them to the Holland River and north again to Lake Simcoe, where goods could be off-loaded at Kempenfelt Bay, where Barrie now lies. From the bay there was a short nine-mile portage to Willow Creek, the Nottawasaga River, and downstream to the southern extremity of Lake Huron.[7]

Large canoes could bring a large amount of goods through the rocky portages of the Ottawa and French rivers, and then risk exposure to the whims of some of the world's largest freshwater lakes. While the second route was slower, it was also more reliable. The third route was even more inconvenient than the lazy lake route. The North West

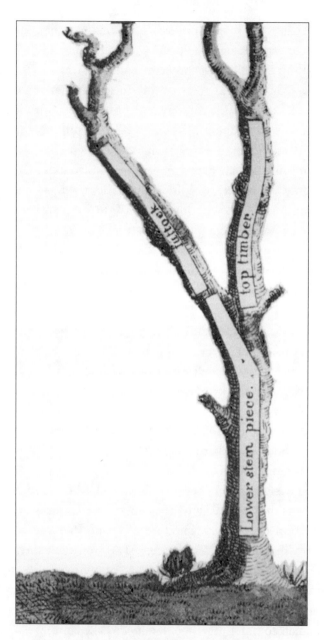

When building wooden sailing vessels shipbuilders found it easier and more desirable to use different parts of the tree for various sections of a ship's hull and masts. In the late eighteenth century Detroit constituted the unrivalled shipbuilding yard and port on the upper Great Lakes. Detroit shipwrights selected and cut timbers for the *Nancy* using some of the techniques shown here. ("Instructions for cutting ship's timbers," from Peter Guillet, *The Timber Merchant's Guide*, Baltimore, 1823 / Peabody Essex Museum.)

Company, reliant on dependable transportation for its trade goods and valuable fur cargoes, used all three. For the last two routes especially, it needed sailing boats on the water to haul its commerce over the freshwater seas. These boats had to be small enough to negotiate the shallow waters of the lake harbours, estuaries and rivers, but also hardy enough to sustain operation in the rough, unpredictable weather of the lakes.

From the time of her launching, the *Nancy* sailed in waters surrounded mostly by untouched wilderness. Her birthplace of Detroit was the largest urban centre of the interior. Founded in 1701 by French administrator Cadillac, Detroit slowly grew as the French built it as a fur-trading centre. Ottawas, Wyandots, Potowatomi, Ojibways and Mississaugas all traded with the French, and eventually a fort and some agricultural infrastructure were built around the fledgling fur-trading community.[8]

After 1783, Detroit and everything south of Lake Erie, west of Lake Huron and east of the Niagara River was officially American territory. Michilimackinac, hub of the Northwestern fur trade, came into American hands, and the British responded by building a ramshackle outpost on nearby St. Joseph's Island. Black Rock and Buffalo, opposite the British guns at Fort Erie, were the scene of some commercial activity. Presqu'isle, now Erie, Pennsylvania, protected by a sandbar, was a small harbour town with a population of just over four hundred. Further to the west lay a straggling string of settlements along the small creeks and rivers that poured into Lake Erie — Cleveland, for instance, had a population of only forty-seven people.[9] It was only at the far western end of Lake Erie, where the French-Canadian settlements in lower Michigan began, that any kind of significant, permanent lakeside settlement occurred before Detroit.

The Canadian side of the lakes was even more sparsely populated. There were small communities around the British forts at Amherstburg and Fort Erie. Just after the turn of the nineteenth century, Colonel John Talbot had brought in settlers from Ireland, and farming communities were beginning to spring up around the mouth of the Grand River just west of the Niagara Peninsula. The overland route along the Niagara River was perhaps the best populated, but westward there was only one

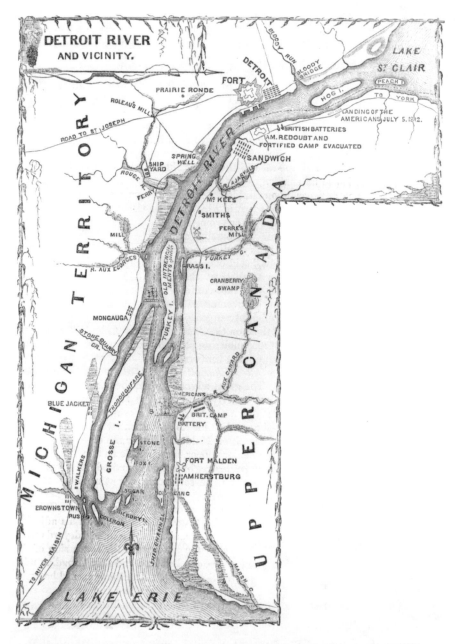

This enlarged view of the Detroit River shows the relative positions of Forts Detroit and Malden and the villages of Detroit, Sandwich and Amherstburg. Notice the position of the Detroit shipyard, on the Rouge River south west of Detroit. This prosperous agricultural and fur-trading region became a hotly contested battleground during the War of 1812. ("Detroit River and Vicinity" / From B.J. Lossing, *Pictorial Field-Book of the War of 1812*, New York, 1869 / Library and Archives Canada / C-010739)

very rough road that struggled along Lake Erie's north shore to Amherstburg. Along the St. Clair River banks were other small settlements and scattered farms. North of Sandwich, however, no major port or base existed along all of Lake Huron until the very northern tip of the lake, where the fur-trading depots and military barracks of St. Joseph's Island and St. Mary's could be found near the rapids of Sault Ste. Marie.[10]

The difference between the American and the Canadian sides of the lake was one of depth. Once the initial wilderness was penetrated to the south, the American states became populated and prosperous. Pittsburgh, the modern steel city, was already, by 1812, a bustling manufacturing city with a population of around six thousand people.[11] The American westward expansion had already begun, and the new state of Ohio was filling with frontier farmers and a growing commercial base. By the time war was declared, Ohio alone had a population of over 230,000 people.[12]

Upper Canada had no such depth. With a total population of only around 75,000, and most of these in the eastern areas around Kingston, Upper Canada did not have the vast American reservoirs of manpower and industrial output.[13] Instead, its links to the wider world were to the east, via the St. Lawrence to the shipping centres of Montreal, Quebec and Halifax. These routes required energy and resourcefulness to maintain, and determination to defend.

As the *Nancy* glided through the inland seas, her decks laden with trade goods of the North West Company, none of these inequalities would have been very apparent. From Fort Erie to the St. Clair River and beyond, the shoreline appeared as a long line of rocks, trees and swamp, interrupted only occasionally by the odd farmhouse or settlement.

It was to this wilderness that war came in 1812. While the fur traders had peddled their goods via the inland waterways, political tensions between London and Washington had reached breaking point. By the beginning of the nineteenth century, Great Britain was the world's foremost naval power. Locked in an exhausting conflict with Napoleonic France, the ships of the Royal Navy were all that stood between the island nation and the land armies of Napoleon Bonaparte. The Royal Navy blockaded the European coast, cutting off trade with continental France and ensuring the supply to the British army fighting the French in Spain.

To maintain its blockade of France and French allies, Great Britain gave the Royal Navy sweeping permission to seize suspected naval deserters from neutral ships. It also required all neutral ships attempting to land in France to first put in at a British port and declare their cargoes. These British orders-in-council, although aimed at prosecuting the war against France, also trampled on the rights of non-belligerent nations, especially those of the United States.

The young United States was accustomed to asserting its overseas commercial rights. In retaliation for American co-operation with British shipping laws, in 1797 the French government decreed American shipping eligible for confiscation. What resulted has been called the American "quasi-war" with France, a state of undeclared hostility that saw the birth of the United States Navy and much American success against French shipping.

A temporary peace between Great Britain and France in 1801 led to an end of the quasi-war. However, the Americans almost immediately sent their new navy on what turned into a four-year expedition against the Barbary pirates. From 1801 to 1805 the United States Navy engaged the forces of the dey of Algiers in an effort to end attacks on American shipping. An assault on the North African town of Derna in 1805 forced the Algerian pirates into a peace and friendship treaty with the United States.[14]

The peace between Great Britain and France did not last long. By 1805 the two great powers were again at war, and it was in October of that year that Britain crushed its opponent's sea power. At the battle of Trafalgar, the Royal Navy smashed a combined French and Spanish fleet and claimed total mastery of the sea for Great Britain. Napoleon reacted in 1807 by prohibiting most of continental Europe from trading with the British. Great Britain was forced to enact its orders-in-council infringing on American and other neutral maritime rights.

Relations between Great Britain and the United States steadily deteriorated from that point. In 1807, HMS *Leopard* opened fire on USS *Chesapeake* when the American ship refused to be searched. The engagement, which took place off Norfolk, killed three American seamen, wounded eighteen others and resulted in four being pressed into the Royal Navy. Americans were shocked and outraged, but despite some calls for war, the United States government hesitated. The United States eventually responded with the Embargo Act, and later the Non-Intercourse Act, which prohibited trade with Great Britain and France. In 1811 another collision took place, not far from the scene of *Chesapeake*'s humiliation. USS *President* attacked HMS *Little Belt* in retaliation for the impressments of American sailors, and dragged the two countries ever closer to war.[15]

Events in the North American interior also helped set the two nations on a collision course. In November 1811 a mixture of American regular and militia troops attacked an allied force of Natives camped on the banks of the Tippecanoe River in Indiana territory. The so-called Battle of Tippecanoe was the culmination of a long series of skirmishes between American regulars and frontier militia and a growing Native confederacy led by the Shawnee chief Tecumseh and his half-brother the Prophet.

Tecumseh and the Prophet had been organizing an alliance of Native bands to resist American westward expansion. Frontier leaders in the United States suspected Great Britain of providing encouragement, arms and ammunition to the Natives through the British Indian Department and various fur-trading companies. British fur traders, like those of the North West Company, were especially suspected as having great influence and control over the Natives of the Northwest. The North West Company, although based in Montreal, used the extended rivers and lakes of the New World to push a fur-trading empire up the Ottawa River, through lakes Huron and Superior and out into the upper Mississippi, and beyond. Their trade with the northwestern Native nations, as well as the gifts and presents handed out by the British Indian Department, helped funnel supplies, arms and ammunition to the American frontier. The Americans thus laid the blame for Native militancy at the feet of Great Britain and their agents in Canada.[16]

In June 1812, President James Madison declared war on Great Britain. Citing British abuses at sea and in the interior, the United States mobilized its armed forces. With their commercial connections in the United States, the North West Company soon learned of the declaration. The news spread from Washington to Quebec, and by 1 July, as the *Nancy* lay bobbing peacefully at home anchorage, news of the declaration of war raced up the Detroit River.[17]

The charismatic Shawnee chief Tecumseh led a coalition of Native forces against the Americans before and during the War of 1812. He worked closely with Generals Isaac Brock and Henry Procter, although his relationship is said to have been better with the former. Killed at the battle of Moraviantown on 5 October 1813, Tecumseh's death led to a near disintegration of the Native coalition. ("Portrait of Tecumseh," from B.J. Lossing, *Pictorial Field-Book of the War of 1812*)

While the *Nancy* was armed, she was not built for war. This was the age of black-powder warfare, when massive iron cannon were used to hurl heavy iron shot to destroy an enemy. Warships, then as now, are weapons carriers, and in the age of fighting sail they were floating gun platforms, designed to carry as many guns as possible and crammed with men to fire them. At the time, they primarily carried two kinds of cannon. The long gun was the traditional armament. Long, thick-barrelled and extremely heavy, these cannon could accurately fire shot over long ranges. They were mounted on wheeled trucks for easier handling. The carronade was a shorter, stubbier version of its long cousin. Mounted on a sliding rail to keep its size down, it was smaller and lighter, with a thinner barrel than the long gun. What the carronade lacked in size and accuracy, it gained in brute force and was known in the British Navy as "the smasher."

Both forms of cannon fired a variety of shot. Solid shot was for destroying hulls and masts. Chain shot — two round shot, or similar items, chained together by forged iron links — rotated in the air as it thundered toward its targets. Chain shot was used to destroy sails and rigging. Grapeshot — cast-iron balls arranged in a tier so as to have a destructive spread — was used to incapacitate men.

All forms of cannon, whether based at sea or on land, were classified by the weight of shot they fired. The two small six-pound guns the *Nancy* mounted on her exposed decks fired iron balls weighing six pounds each. *Nancy* was built to carry cargo, and to be worked by as few men as possible. In the event of war, she would be easily overmatched by warships carrying twelve-, eighteen- or twenty-four-pound guns.

Although they were a vital link in communications and in the fur trade, neither American nor British authorities had devoted much thought to war on the Great Lakes. Both sides concentrated their navies on the Atlantic seaboard, not the inland waterways. The British command on the lakes boasted only a motley collection of Provincial Marine vessels. The Provincial Marine was not part of the regular Royal Navy, but was rather a separate entity maintained by the Quartermaster General's Office to ferry supplies and troops as required. Even this relatively benign existence was not enough to keep the Provincial Marine busy all the time. When there was not enough military work to be done, the Provincial Marine was occasionally hired out as a transportation option for the local fur traders.[18]

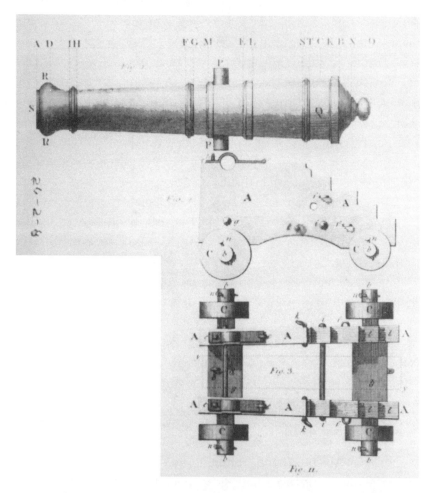

Carriages such as these held the long-gun form of naval cannon. Long guns had greater range and accuracy than carronades but had less "stopping power." During the War of 1812 these cannons armed not only large warships, but also forts and other land batteries. ("Iron Guns for the Navy," artist unknown / Naval Historical Center / US Navy)

By 1812, the Provincial Marine was in a sorry state. Between lakes Ontario and Erie, it had a total of seven vessels. The Lake Erie division was particularly falling into disrepair. The brig *Camden* was "[d]eclared by a board of survey to be incapable of going to sea & even unfit to lodge the seamen during winter." The other vessels, the sixteen-gun ship *Queen Charlotte* and the six-gun schooner *General Hunter*, were serviceable, but the *General Hunter* was "fast falling into decay."[19]

The Lake Erie division also had some unique geographical problems to surmount. The St. Clair River was the only means of water communication between lakes Erie and Huron. Any war vessels that were to operate on both lakes had to have a shallow enough draft to be able to navigate the sometimes shallow and unpredictable waters of the river. A shallow draft meant that the vessel had to be smaller, with fewer guns and less cargo room than a vessel with a deeper draft. Of the Provincial Marine division on Lake Erie, only the six-gun schooner *General Hunter* could navigate the river. As a result, there were recommendations for a new schooner to be built at Amherstburg to bolster the dilapidated fleet.[20] Another schooner, *Lady Prevost*, was laid down and slated to be completed by July 1812.

The Lake Ontario division was headquartered at Kingston and was only in slightly better shape. It consisted of the twenty-gun ship *Royal George*, the brig *Moira* and the six-gun schooner *Duke of Gloucester*. A fourth vessel, the *Duke of Kent*, was listed as being "solely used in Winter as a barrack for the seamen & incapable of repair."[21] Another schooner, the *Prince Regent*, was being built at York and, like the *Lady Prevost*, was to be ready by the summer of 1812.

If the small number of lake vessels seemed inadequate, so did their commanders. Captain Alexander Grant commanded the Lake Ontario division. An astute old sailor, Grant could see the war coming and asked to be given retirement in England to make way for younger, more energetic officers. The stubborn Captain Steel, however, commanded Lake Erie. Steel, eighty-seven years old and reaching his limits commanding even an entity as basic as the Provincial Marine, flatly refused to step aside. Deputy Quartermaster Captain Andrew Gray wrote to the British commander in North America, Lieutenant General Sir George Prevost, recommending that Steel "…should be

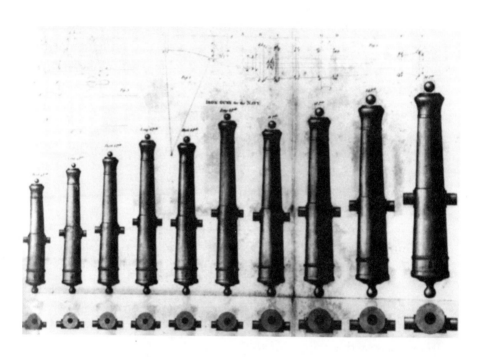

A variety of gun sizes existed to navies during the War of 1812. These different sized guns each fired a different sized shot, and required varying amounts of powder. This variety meant that the supply systems for both sides in the conflict had to be sophisticated enough to get the right sized ammunition to the right sized guns at the right locations. ("Iron Guns for the Navy," artist unknown / Naval Historical Center / US Navy)

removed, as he cannot be of any service; but may possibly do harm, by standing in the way of others."[22]

The Provincial Marine also faced stiff competition for sailors from the private transportation companies on the lakes. Experienced sailors could earn considerably more money working for the fur traders or private ship owners than they could in the service of king and country. Provincial Marine sailors could earn extra money by becoming part of the manual labour force employed in the naval dockyards at Kingston or Amherstburg. This "working money" became a disincentive, however, as the most capable seamen were retained on the vessels, and the least capable were sent ashore to work in the marine yards. For a competent sailor on the lakes, the Provincial Marine not only paid lower wages than the private merchants, but was also bound not to let them make up the difference by earning extra cash ashore. Taken together, these factors gave the Provincial Marine great problems in maintaining itself as a fighting force.

If the British lake fleets seemed small, unprepared and inadequate, the United States Navy's flotillas were even worse. The only armed American vessel west of Niagara was the fourteen-gun brig *Adams*, stationed at Detroit. *Adams*, like her Provincial Marine counterparts, spent most of her time running supplies to isolated military outposts on the upper Great Lakes. She was seriously outgunned by the little Provincial Marine fleet across the river at Amherstburg, although she did have the ability to run up under the guns of the fortress at Detroit.[23]

On Lake Ontario, the Americans were similarly at a disadvantage. They possessed only the brig *Oneida*, commanded by Lieutenant Melancthon Woolsey. *Oneida* was little more than a coast guard vessel, and was mostly employed in embargo enforcement. When news of war finally reached its commander, he immediately doubled the American fleet on that lake by pressing the schooner *Lord Nelson* into the American service. Woolsey had confiscated *Lord Nelson* on suspicion of smuggling; now he used the former embargo-runner to try and even his odds against the British.[24]

Both the British and American lake navies could call upon commercial vessels to fill out their squadrons. Vessels like the *Nancy* could be impressed into service and armed as warships. Although not designed

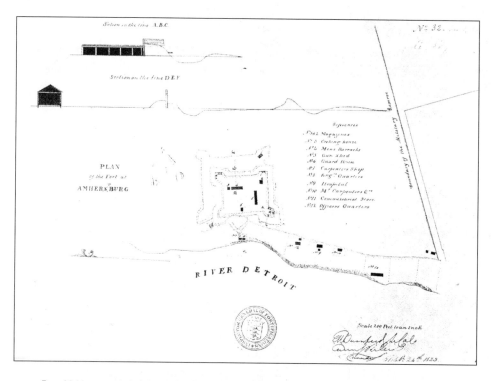

Fort Malden guarded the mouth of the Detroit River near the town of Amherstburg, Upper Canada. The fort had fallen into disrepair in the early part of the nineteenth century, but in the spring of 1812 the British worked hard to repair its ramparts and palisades. Some of Fort Malden's guns armed Commodore Barclay's fleet during the Battle of Put-in-Bay, 10 September 1813. ("Plan of Fort Malden," by E.W. Durnford / National Archives of Canada / NMC 4553)

for warfare, they could be armed with an assortment of weapons to make them at least capable of defending themselves against an equal opponent in a lake action.

The British possessed an advantage in this floating reserve in the form of the North West Company. Because of the intensely competitive and sometimes violent nature of the fur trade, the North West Company already had two vessels on Lake Superior, the *Perseverance* and *Mink*. The smaller *Mink*, at only 60 tons, could be run over the rapids at Sault Ste. Marie and brought down into Lake Huron. The North West Company also had two armed vessels at Sandwich, on the St. Clair River: the *Nancy* and the *Caledonia*. At the war's opening, each of these supported four guns.[25] On 1 July, with news of war, the *Nancy* quickly ran downstream to the British fortifications at Amherstburg, where British guns could protect her from becoming an early prize.[26]

The North West Company and its employees were ready to take action for the preservation of Upper Canada. Because all their supply routes ran from Montreal through one or all of the Great Lakes, the maintenance of British superiority, especially on Lake Huron, was of the foremost importance in keeping the fur-trade business open. In January 1812 the fur traders offered their full military support to the defence of Canada. "The Heads of the Companies are exceedingly grateful to your Excellency for taking an interest in the protection of their Trade that they will enter with zeal into any measures of Defence, *or even Offence* that may be proposed to them," Gray wrote to Prevost. "They have tendered all their Vessels for the service of the Gov't if the exigencies of the war should make it necessary to call for them — In short they are full of Loyalty and zeal, and manifest a degree of public spirit highly honourable to them."[27] The North West Company's offer of military support naturally included turning the *Nancy* into a warship.

The British were of two minds on how to hold Canada against an American invasion. The first viewpoint belonged to Sir George Prevost, the British Empire's most powerful figure in North America. Prevost had been made commander-in-chief of the British forces in North America and governor of British North America in 1811. His military command responsibilities stretched from Upper and Lower Canada to New Brunswick, Nova Scotia, Newfoundland and even Bermuda.[28] His

Sir George Prevost served as the overall British administrator and military commander in North America. Bilingual, diplomatic, and an experienced army officer, Prevost directed British strategy from his headquarters at Quebec. Prevost understood the strategic necessity of keeping the Northwest in British hands, and in February 1814 he sent one of his most trusted subordinates, Lieutenant-Colonel Robert McDouall, to command the British garrison at Michilimackinac. Prevost's reputation suffered a grievous and perhaps undeserved blow after his defeat at the Battle of Plattsburgh in 1814. Following the War of 1812 Prevost requested a court-martial so he could publicly explain his actions at the battle. He died, however, one week before the court could convene. ("Sir George Prevost," artist Charles William Jefferys / Library and Archives Canada / C-70392)

father had been a Swiss volunteer in the British Army and had fought under the victorious Wolfe at the Plains of Abraham. Prevost himself had served in a number of regiments and had been wounded in action on the island of St. Vincent. In 1798 he was promoted to brigadier general. After successfully defending several Caribbean colonies from French attacks, he was transferred back to North America as governor of Nova Scotia in 1808.[29]

Throughout his career, Prevost had shown himself to be a bold and capable military commander and a shrewd administrator. His actions in the Caribbean won him acclaim and a baronetcy in 1805. He was also completely fluent in French, a distinct advantage to a British administrator in mostly French Lower Canada. With his new and extended command, however, Prevost faced a discouraging strategic situation. While Nova Scotia had the British naval base at Halifax, Prevost only had about six thousand regular troops to defend both Upper and Lower Canada.[30]

Since these two provinces were the most likely targets of an American invasion, Prevost had to think hard about his priorities. Upper Canada was sparsely populated, difficult of access, supply and reinforce, and was exposed to American offensives across the St. Clair, Niagara and St. Lawrence rivers. Its population was a mixed bag of French-Canadians, various Native nations, British émigrés, and recent American immigrants. This last group, with their possible sympathies to an invading American force, worried the British administrators the most. Lower Canada, by contrast, was only accessible to the American invaders either by the Lake Champlain–Richelieu River route, or the St. Lawrence. It could be supplied by the Royal Navy — at least while there was no ice — and was buttressed by the old stone fortress at Quebec itself.

To compound matters, Prevost had been ordered by London to refrain from any offensive operations that would jeopardize peace talks and extend the war with the United States any further than was necessary. Under the circumstances, Prevost adopted a defensive strategy, and was prepared to sacrifice his strung-out line in Upper Canada for a more compact and defensible position around Montreal and Quebec City. Given the vulnerability and isolation of most of the British posts

In 1812 Major General Isaac Brock, British military commander and civil governor in Upper Canada, advocated an offensive strategy for the war. He ordered the attack on Michilimackinac in July 1812 and orchestrated the British victory at Detroit in August. Brock reportedly earned the respect of the Native leader Tecumseh. The British government awarded Brock a knighthood for his actions at Detroit, but he was killed at the battle of Queenston Heights before he could receive the honour. For his defence of Upper Canada, Brock became a hero in Canadian history and today a large monument stands to his honour at Queenston, Ontario. ("Sir Isaac Brock," artist John Wycliffe Lowes Forster / Library and Archives Canada / C-007760)

west of Kingston, and given the military potential of the States south of the wilderness belt, Prevost was reluctant to commit men and materiel to Upper Canada.[31]

Even the North West Company, which relied on the Great Lakes for the vitality of its business, admitted that holding the St. Clair River was an impossibility and recommended falling back on the York–Lake Simcoe supply line.[32] In fact, despite their brave face in offering help to the British commanders, the North West Company was privately preparing for the worst. At their annual meeting at Fort William in 1812, the company's partners agreed to send men to the company depot at Lac La Pluie to bring as many furs out of the Northwest via the French River route as quickly as possible. They also began stockpiling arms and ammunition at the locks at Sault Ste. Marie, so that their agents could "...act as circumstances require."[33] It was also suggested that the outposts in the interior begin stocking up in case supplies from Montreal were cut off. Upper Canada seemed doomed, even to those who were most prepared to defend it.

The second mind on Upper Canada's defence belonged to Major General Sir Isaac Brock. Born to a landholding family on the Channel Island of Guernsey, Brock was a career military officer. He had commanded his infantry regiment, the 49th, in operations in the Netherlands and at Nelson's attack on Copenhagen. By 1812 he was the civilian and military commander in Upper Canada, second only to Sir George Prevost in Quebec. Brock was also fluently bilingual, diplomatic and charismatic. His strong working relationship with the Native leader Tecumseh has become legendary, and it permitted many of the successful operations in 1812.

Charged with planning the defence of Upper Canada, Brock realized that the key to holding the province was to seize and hold the American Northwest. The area around the naval base of Amherstburg was "the most important, and if supplied with the means of commencing active operations, must deter the Americans from any offensive attempt from Niagara westward." He assured Prevost that control of the Lake Erie–Lake Huron area would force the Americans to "secure their western frontier from the inroads of the Indians, and this cannot be effected without very considerable force.... But before we can expect an active co-operation on the part of the Indians, the reduction of Detroit and Michilimackinac, must convince the people … that we are earnestly engaged in the War."[34] Brock wanted to hit the Americans hard and fast in the west, to tie up as many of their forces there as possible and divert them from operations against the rest of Upper Canada. This offensive strategy also meant bringing the Native nations into the war on the British side, an essential reinforcement to the very small numbers of British troops that were stationed in the province.

For their part, American offensive plans for 1812 involved a three-pronged attack. The first was to be a strike across the St. Clair River from Detroit, capturing the communications between the upper and lower Great Lakes and then pushing eastward through the province. The second was to similarly strike across the Niagara River, cutting access between lakes Ontario and Erie, and possibly linking with the force from Detroit somewhere around Burlington, near the west end of Lake Ontario. The third prong was to strike north to Montreal, up the Richelieu River valley, and deliver the *coup de grâce* against Lower Canada. By capturing Montreal, the Americans would cut all supplies and communications west of Quebec City and would guarantee the conquest of the province. It was this third strike that concerned the British, especially Prevost, the most. With a single blow, the Americans could totally sever Upper Canada, and the fur trade west of Upper Canada, from the British Empire.

Both the British and Americans knew that control of the lakes would be the key to success. All of Brock's offensive plans were predicated on controlling the water access points into Michigan. "From Amherstburg to Fort Erie my chief dependence must rest on a naval force for the protection of that extensive coast," Brock wrote. "If consequently the Garrison of St. Joseph's is to be maintained, and an attack on Michilimackinac undertaken, it will be expedient to hire or purchase from the Merchants, as many vessels as may be necessary for the purpose."[35] In order for Brock's thrust at the American Northwest to work, the Provincial Marine would have to completely control Lake Erie and, by extension, Lake Huron. Failure to do so would isolate the British troops at the end of very uncertain, and in some cases nonexistent, supply lines, and lead to defeat in the west and the prospect of facing the concentrated thrusts of massive American invasion forces.

For the Americans, control of the waterways was equally important. Their isolated garrison at Michilimackinac could only be serviced by the *Adams* or the handful of commercial vessels on the lakes. Detroit itself was most easily accessed by water — the only other route was a rough track hacked out of the wilderness to the Miami River. From there, an enterprising soul could travel through a maze of rivers to the populous centres of Ohio or Pennsylvania. Cutting overland through the swamps and forests of lakeside Ohio and Michigan was not the preferred route to Detroit. But with even the modest Provincial Marine prowling the lakes, the American Army of the Northwest had no choice. As war loomed, the Americans blazed a track through the Black Swamp, linking Urbana, Ohio, with the Miami rapids and the difficult road north to Detroit.[36]

The first prong of the American invasion of Canada was launched on 12 July 1812. General William Hull crossed the St. Clair River with a collection of regular forces and militia from Ohio, Kentucky and Michigan — in all, roughly two thousand men. Hull was a lawyer by training but had served in the Continental Army during the American Revolution, where he earned a reputation for daring. In 1805 Hull was made governor of the Michigan Territory. There he negotiated settlements with several Native tribes and tried to bolster Michigan's defence system as war loomed with Great Britain. Despite his advancing age and failing health, he was in 1812 made a brigadier general and put in charge of a mixed force of militia and regular units from the Northwestern United States.[37] It was with this Army of the Northwest that Hull and his subordinates had tramped through the woods and swamps on the rough track to Detroit. It was with this army that they aimed to conquer western Upper Canada.

The militia of Essex and Kent counties found themselves in a difficult position. In total, they numbered no more than six hundred men — far too few to take on Hull's invasion force. As early as 5 July the militiamen had become anxious watching the American preparations. On that day, Hull opened a short barrage with a four-pound gun and a massive twenty-four-pound gun. Several of the twenty-four-pound shot

HULL IN FORT DETROIT.

Brigadier General William Hull, a lawyer by training, held various commands in the Continental Army during the War of the American Revolution. In 1812 he was governor of the Michigan Territory and commander of the American army of the Northwest. Plagued by numerous supply and communications problems, Hull briefly occupied the Upper Canadian town of Sandwich; however, after hearing of the loss of Michilimackinac he withdrew to Detroit. Hull then surrendered Detroit and the Michigan Territory to Brock on 16 August 1812. Later being court-martialled and found guilty of cowardice and neglect of duty, Hull received a pardon from President James Madison for his former services. ("Hull in Fort Detroit," artist Felix O. C. Darley / Library and Archives Canada / C-008982) smashed into a house in Sandwich, and the militia sent word to Amherstburg that the invasion was imminent. St. George tried to calm the panicky militia by promising to reinforce them when the Americans crossed the river. After another three days of waiting, the suspense was too much for the Essex and Kent militia to bear; on 8 July, concerned that so many of his anxious men wanted to return home, Colonel François Baby ordered his militiamen to move to Amherstburg. They had reached the Canard River, just north of Fort Malden, when St. George countermanded the order and sent them back to Sandwich, this time backed up by fifty men of the 41st Regiment and a pair of three-pound field guns.[38]

Even with reinforcements, it was clear that the militia position in Sandwich was untenable. The militiamen were not professional soldiers. They had businesses and, more importantly, farms to attend to. For the latter, July was a critical time; it was in mid-month that the crops were normally ready for harvesting. In a part of the province which was used to only slim food surpluses, the tending to planted fields was a matter of survival; attention to militia service was secondary. After five days of waiting in Sandwich, the militia was anxious and restless. On 11 July, Baby once again decided to withdraw to Fort Malden. Colonel St. George held that the militia would desert in the night if they were not kept close to the regular troops, and agreed to the move.[39] When Hull's troops landed on the Canadian shore the next day, they found Sandwich undefended.

After crossing into Canada, he issued a proclamation offering friendship to the local residents. His language seems to be that of the liberator, not the conqueror. "Inhabitants of Canada!" the declaration pronounced. "The army under my Command has invaded your Country and the standard of the United States waves on the territory of Canada. To the peaceable and unoffending inhabitant, it brings neither danger nor difficulty. I come to *find* enemies, not to *make* them, I come to *protect* not to *injure* you." He promised to protect private property and to uphold the rights of the locals. He also declared, "No white man found fighting by the side of an Indian will be taken prisoner."[40]

Hull had hoped that the proclamation would deter the local Upper Canadians from fighting for the British. He was right. When Hull first crossed the Detroit River, the Essex Flank companies turned out to bolster the British regulars and the local Native warriors. But as days wore on and there was no fighting, the militia's numbers began to dwindle. Brock reported to Prevost that the local militia "behaved very ill. The officers appear the most in fault.... Were it possible to animate the militia to a proper sense of their duty something might yet be done, but I almost despair."[41] Indeed, the militia did not come out to defend their province for king and country. When Hull crossed the river, 360 local militiamen gave their paroles to the American forces, and on 17 July, when Ohio militia commander Duncan McArthur returned from a foraging expedition up the Thames River, he brought back the paroles of the upriver residents as well.[42] The war had come, and most residents were content to stay out of it.

As the prospects for a successful defence diminished hourly, the British commander at Amherstburg, Lieutenant Colonel St. George of the 41st Regiment, began begging for reinforcements. Brock, who was wrestling with the Upper Canadian legislature on the issue of martial law and other wartime precautions, was worried that a more energetic enemy attack would hit Upper Canada at Niagara or Kingston. As a result, he could only spare small numbers of troops for the west until he was sure that the vital points in the east would be safe, at least temporarily, from attack.

At Amherstburg, the *Nancy* joined the war effort. The four small guns the North West Company had given her were taken away to arm gunboats patrolling the river. The *Nancy* and the Provincial Marine schooner *Lady Prevost* were sent to Fort Erie on 30 July to pick up reinforcements. There, the *Nancy* was jammed with sixty soldiers of the 41st Regiment before returning to Amherstburg without incident. The Americans in Buffalo noted her presence, and a local paper, the *Buffalo Gazette*, announced her trip back to Amherstburg under the escort of the armed Provincial Marine brig *General Hunter*.[43]

This vital reinforcement was part of a growing stream of fresh troops for the defence of Amherstburg. The little *Nancy* was providing invaluable service as a means of keeping Amherstburg alive while Hull indecisively moved his troops back and forth across the St. Clair River. Hull was in an unenviable position: as long as the Provincial Marine held control of Lake Erie, the British could use ships such as the *Nancy* to bring in fresh troops and supplies. Without such command of the lake, Hull's only supply route was a rough track through the wilderness to the Miami rapids, fifty miles to the south. From the Miami, it was still a tough overland haul through the Black Swamp or up the unpredictable Auglaize or Sandusky River before anything could reach the infrastructure of inner Ohio.[44] Hull could form no concentrated plan of attack on Amherstburg and he worried about his lines of retreat and supply back to the United States.

On 2 August news of the capture of the garrison at Fort Michilimackinac reached Detroit. Shortly after the declaration of war, Brock had ordered Captain Charles Roberts, the commandant at St. Joseph's Island, to commence operations against Michilimackinac. Roberts was in a weak position himself. He had with him only a handful of men from the 10th Royal Veterans battalion, a sort of convalescent unit for men too old or ineffectual for front-line duty. Their primary job had been to act as sort of security guards on the little island just to the southeast of modern Sault Ste. Marie. Their years of isolation and boredom had done little improve the state of the British troops. They were far from being a menacing force. By himself, there was little Roberts could do to reach Michilmackinac, let alone storm the American fortress.

Fortunately for Roberts, the North West Company was true to its word. It did not take long for the company to amass an army of fur trade–hardened voyageurs and pack them into their armed little schooner *Caledonia*. As a long-standing business partner with many of the Native nations in the area, the North West Company also sent its agents out looking for military support from Native communities around the upper Great Lakes. Robert Dickson, an experienced and respected fur trader, had already been in contact with General Brock about enlisting Native allies. Under Dickson's urging, eager Native warriors swarmed to St. Joseph's to aid in the British war effort. As June turned into July, Roberts found himself transformed from the commandant of a backwater post into the general of a swelling multinational army under the Union Jack.

At ten o'clock on the morning of 16 July, Captain Charles Roberts embarked his little army in a flotilla of canoes. In all, he had 180 North

MICHILIMACKINAC ON LAKE HURON.

To his Excellency Sir George Prevost Bar.   Governor General and Commander in Chief
of all his Majesties Forces   in British America.
THIS PRINT is humbly Inscribed by his Excellency   most obedient humble Servant RICHARD DILLON JUN.

The island fort of Michilimackinac held the key to diplomatic relations with Native nations north and west of lakes Huron, Superior and Michigan. The vessel shown here is the *Nancy*. In a brilliant, bloodless victory, British and allied forces captured Michilimackinac on 17 July 1812. In August 1814 American forces under Commodore Arthur Sinclair attempted to recapture this strategic location. After a bloody land battle, American forces retreated and Sinclair prepared to leave Lake Huron. After destroying the *Nancy*, Sinclair despatched two of his vessels to blockade Michilimackinac. British forces under Lieutenant Worsley, Royal Navy, captured both these American vessels, completing the U.S. Navy's losses on Lake Huron. ("Michilimackinac," artist Richard Dillon / McCord Museum / M3954)

West voyageurs, 400 Natives and 45 soldiers from the 10th Royal Veterans. Led by the North West Company's brig *Caledonia*, Roberts's force headed west toward American waters and the fur-trade fortress of Michilimackinac.

Michilimackinac was a lonely outpost. An island three miles long and two across, it was abutted at its eastern end by a series of blunt cliffs. It tapered slowly to the west by tough, wooded slopes, and ended in a small bay. Settlers and fur traders had built a modest village not far from the island's fort, on the southeastern coast. The fort was a weak log structure, overshadowed by Michilimackinac's ominous western end. But the island itself was strong. It commanded all communication, and the entire fur trade, west into Lake Michigan and beyond. It was the key gateway to the Northwest.[45]

The fortress was commanded by Lieutenant Porter Hanks of the United States Artillery Regiment. The afternoon of 16 July, an Indian interpreter in town told Hanks that there was some talk among the local Natives that a strong force was massing at St. Joseph's Island to attack Michilimackinac. Hanks, unsure what to make of the rumour, ordered Captain Michael Dousman of the local militia to go to St. Joseph's Island and find out what the Natives there were up to. Dousman set off in a canoe that night, but got only a dozen miles before he found himself surrounded by Roberts's flotilla. Dousman was quickly captured and brought along with the invasion force.[46]

At three o'clock on the morning of 17 July, "By the almost unparalleled exertions of the Canadians who manned the Boats,"[47] Roberts's men landed on the American island. Michael Dousman was then told to gather up the civilians in the town quietly and lead them to the west side of the island, where they would be protected by a British guard. Dousman was warned not to alert the American authorities, but while he was organizing the evacuation the local physician, Dr. Day, quietly slipped into the fort and told Hanks the island was under attack. Hanks immediately stockpiled ammunition and ordered his men to their posts.[48] Meanwhile, the mixed British-Native-North West Company force dragged a small six-pounder gun to the heights overlooking the American fort. The Native warriors surrounded the American position. At ten o'clock, exactly twenty-four hours after leaving St. Joseph's, Captain Charles Roberts issued his demand for the Americans to surrender Michilimackinac.[49]

Inside the flimsy wooden stockade, Hanks had few options. He had only sixty-one men under his command. Four were unfit for duty, and another five were musicians and not really trained to defend the fort against an army of armed Natives and fur traders.[50] When Hanks had gone to bed the night before, he had been unaware that war had even been declared.[51] Now he was surrounded by British soldiers, Native warriors and Canadian militia. An American civilian who had carried Roberts's demand into the American fort explained that the British numbered nearly a thousand, and that they had brought scaling ladders and ropes with which to climb over the walls of the fort.[52]

Roberts offered Hanks generous terms of surrender. The garrison would be permitted to march out of the fort and surrender with full honour. Roberts promised to do as much as he could to protect the private property of the local inhabitants, and the fur-trade vessels in the harbour were to remain private property. The people of Michilimackinac would have to swear an oath of allegiance to the British crown, but any who refused would be given a month to pack their things and leave the island. Finally, Hanks's men would be paroled — that is, they would be considered prisoners of war but would be allowed to return to the United States.[53] They could not serve against the British until they were formally permitted to do so by an "exchange" organized by delegates from the two countries. It meant that while Hanks's men could not fight until their "release," they could serve their time in the comfort of the United States and be spared time in a British prison. They were generous terms, and Hanks had no other option. An hour later, at eleven o'clock in the morning, Hanks surrendered the fort. The British colours were hoisted above Michilmackinac and the first encounter of the War of 1812 ended without a shot being fired.

Roberts and his men were true to their word. Private property in Michilimackinac was respected, and so were the lives of the surrendered garrison. "It was a fortunate circumstance that the Fort capitulated without firing a single gun," John Askin Jr. reported. "For if they had done so, I firmly believe not a soul of them would have been saved." Askin knew full well the depth of Native resentment toward the Americans. His father,

John Sr., was the foremost North West Company trader at Amherstburg, and an associate of Angus Mackintosh. John Jr.'s sons helped him control the Native warriors, and in the aftermath of the capitulation, the Natives did not "even kill a Fowl belonging to any person."[54]

When the dejected parolees of Michilimackinac arrived in Detroit a week later, news of the fort's capture stunned the Army of the Northwest. The loss of Michilimackinac meant that the British, the North West Company and their Native allies now controlled the key to the American Northwest. General Hull saw the tide turning against him quickly. He was afraid that hundreds of Native warriors would soon rally to the British cause and descend on isolated American posts, just as they had descended on Michilimackinac. In consequence, Hull immediately ordered the evacuation of the isolated American post of Fort Dearborn (now Chicago).[55] Shortly after ordering the withdrawal from Illinois, Hull himself withdrew across the St. Clair River and back into the safety of the walls of Detroit.

That August, Major General Brock himself arrived at Amherstburg with a collection of militia and regular forces from the vicinities of York and the Grand River. He immediately met with Tecumseh, the architect of the growing Native alliance and charismatic commander of the diverse Native armies. Together they developed a plan to destroy General Hull and the American Army of the Northwest and take control of the upper Great Lakes.

The *Nancy* was a bystander as the army she had laboured so hard to help build was finally put into the field. British regulars, Canadian militia and Native warriors piled into open boats on 16 August. In the crisp pre-dawn darkness, Brock's mixed force began the short row across the Detroit River. A battery of guns set up in front of militia Colonel Francois Baby's house in Sandwich began its bombardment. The Americans in Fort Detroit replied with their own guns, and the artillery duel continued in earnest as Brock's troops drew themselves up about a mile from the American stronghold. When his troops were in position, Brock issued his demand for Hull's surrender. "It was a long time in suspense," Charles Askin, an officer in the Essex militia, wrote at the time. "Many were wishing them to capitulate — there were young Officers who were anxious to have an opportunity of distinguishing

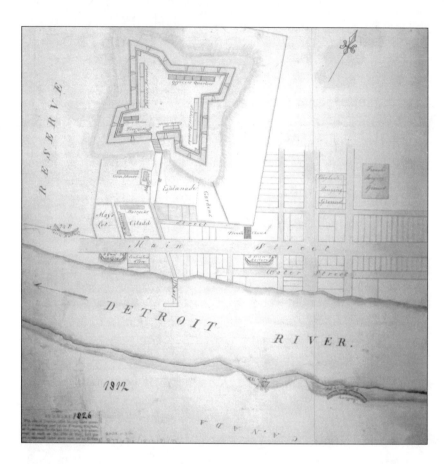

The British built these gun batteries on the Canadian side of the Detroit River and used them to bombard Fort Detroit. The batteries also covered the British crossing of the Detroit River in August 1812. Once in Michigan, the British forces linked up with Tecumseh's Native warriors and surrounded Fort Detroit. American Brigadier General William Hull subsequently surrendered not only Fort Detroit but the whole of the Michigan Territory. ("Plan of Detroit with the batteries constructed in 1812," artist William Evans / Burton Historical Collection, Detroit Public Library)

themselves; but most of us wished I believe they should [surrender] …
to spare the effusion of blood and for the sake of the poor Women and
children who we knew would not be spared by the Indians should an
action once commence."[56] The same thoughts ran through Hull's mind.
After a lengthy deliberation, Brigadier General William Hull surrendered to Isaac Brock.

In the south, the news of the capture of Detroit put Washington
into an uproar. The war, which many had promised would be quick
and easy, had suddenly cost the United States Michilimackinac and
Detroit. Fears of renewed frontier wars with the Native nations were
stirring, and an anxious President Madison called an emergency cabinet
meeting to deal with the deteriorating situation. The war in the interior
had suddenly become serious.[57]

In the north, there was celebration. After leaving Colonel Henry
Procter in command of what was now the British Right Division at
Detroit, Brock returned to central Upper Canada with many of the
British regulars. Procter, who arrived at Amherstburg on 26 July, had
been the commander of the 41st Regiment of Foot and had been in command at Fort George. While St. George had been doing an admirable job,
when the Americans did not attack across the Niagara River, Brock felt
that the situation in the west required the attention of the 41st's commander. Procter had come to Upper Canada ten years earlier, at roughly
the same time as Brock, and the two officers became close.[58]

Like Brock, Procter was a career officer. Born in 1763 the son of a
British army surgeon, he entered the military at age eighteen. He soon
joined the 41st Regiment, and was promoted steadily through the ranks,
receiving command of the regiment as a colonel in 1800. Procter proved
himself a capable commander. Before he took over, the regiment had
been in a sorry state — morale and discipline were poor — and Procter
worked hard to turn it into an effective fighting unit.[59]

Now Procter would need all of his experience to master the situation
in the Northwest. He had few regulars or militia, amended by Native
allies who would fight, but who also needed to be fed and armed. He
was, like Roberts at Michilimackinac, at the very end of the British supply
line, and he was in possession of American territory — territory the
Americans would fight hard to get back.

Brigadier General William Hull surrendered Detroit and the Michigan Territory to Major General Isaac Brock on 16 August 1812. Brock's victory tipped the balance of power in the Northwest to the British side until the fall of 1813. The victory inspired the Natives to follow the British, and forced the Americans to rebuild their army of the Northwest from scratch. ("Hull surrendering to Brock." Burton Historical Collection, Detroit Public Library)

The American prisoners of war were loaded onto all the available lake vessels for transportation to Fort Erie. Alexander Mackintosh and his crew were busy all day bringing more and more men aboard. There were so many prisoners and so little space on the available ships, that conditions were cramped and crowded. To compound the misery, many were sick or suffering from wounds.[60] Somehow, Mackintosh found room in the *Nancy* for 146 American POWs. The *Nancy* set sail on 17 August, along with eleven other vessels, plus smaller open boats. Together they held more than two thousand American regulars and militia — the entire American military force in the Northwest.[61]

Brock himself left that night on board the *Chippawa*.[62] With the capture of Detroit, the Northwest was secure from any immediate American invasions. The same was not true of the Niagara frontier, where Stephen Van Rensselaer was organizing another American army to invade Canada. The *Adams* was renamed the *Detroit* and took her place in the Lake Erie Division of the Provincial Marine. The Americans were now left with no armed vessels above Lake Ontario, and the *Nancy* — and others like her — could run supplies and ammunition without worry.

The state of security did not last long. On 8 October, the ever-resourceful Lieutenant Jesse Elliot, United States Navy, led a combined expedition of armed sailors and soldiers against the *Caledonia* and the freshly renamed *Detroit*. In the early-morning struggle, the American boarding parties managed to cut both brigs out from under the British guns and get the *Caledonia* back to the American shore. During the firefight, the *Detroit* drifted downriver and grounded near Squaw Island in the Niagara River. It was later burned by the Americans. Elliot's daring action demonstrated the still-fluctuating balance of power on the Great Lakes. Brock was the first to appreciate the significance of Elliot's triumph. Shortly after the action, Brock wrote to Prevost: "This event is particularly unfortunate, and may reduce us to incalculable distress. The enemy is making every exertion to gain a naval Superiority on both Lakes which if they accomplish I do not see how we can retain the Country."[63]

A week passed while the Americans gathered their strength. Then a second prong of the American offensive struck across the Niagara River. Led by a bickering and uncooperative mixture of regular and militia officers, the American force landed at Queenston, a small riverside village just upstream from Fort George and Brock's headquarters. Opposed by the professionalism of the flank companies of the 49th Regiment, the American offensive faltered. Only by a turn of luck did the Americans find a way to outflank the defenders. In trying to organize a counterattack Brock was killed, shot just to the left side of this chest. His second-in-command, Colonel Roger Sheaffe, led reinforcements onto the heights and captured the American army.

By the end of 1812, the British had captured two full American armies. They had lost Brock, one of their most energetic and aggressive commanders, but the British still had command of the water. It was an imbalance that Brock knew the Americans were endeavouring to rectify. As the *Nancy* was being laid up for winter, and as the ice slowly began to grip the lakes, the American wilderness began buzzing with new activity. New naval commanders were ordered to the inland lakes, and men were already busy building a brand new fleet designed specifically to smash the Provincial Marine and conquer the inland waterways of North America.

A Shipbuilder's War

*J*ust at the time that news of the capture of Hull's army and the northwestern territories of the United States reached the American capital, President James Madison was on his way to a vacation in the country. When he received the message about the imminent danger posed by the sudden and overwhelming British victory, the president turned his carriage around and headed back down the dusty turnpike to Washington, where he summoned his cabinet. The American government resolved to take complete command of the Great Lakes and recapture the Northwest.[64]

A new commander was chosen for the task of building an American freshwater navy: Isaac Chauncey, then commandant of the New York Navy Yard. "The President of the United States has determined to obtain command of the Lakes Ontario & Erie, with the least possible delay," Paul Hamilton, the U.S. Secretary of the Navy, explained to Chauncey. "You will consider yourself unrestrained … the object must be accomplished; and all the means which you may judge to be essential, must be employed. In addition to the public vessels now on the Lakes — you are at liberty to purchase, hire or build, in your discretion, such others and of such form & armament, as may in your opinion be necessary."[65] Chauncey had carte blanche from the American government to build as big a war fleet as he could.

Work started almost immediately. On the Detroit River, no danger yet existed to British shipping. While the *Nancy* plied the waters

Following the early defeats in the War of 1812, the U.S. Secretary of War sent Commodore Isaac Chauncey to Sacket's Harbour to take command of U.S. naval forces on the Great Lakes. During the War of 1812, Chauncey presided over a massive shipbuilding building campaign on the Great Lakes. Chauncey delegated command of the American Lake Erie squadron first to Captain Oliver Hazard Perry, in 1813, and then to Captain Arthur Sinclair in 1814. ("Commodore Isaac Chauncey," artist Charles William Jefferys / Library and Archives Canada / C-73583)

between Amherstburg and Detroit on behalf of the British army, the Americans began a program to sweep her and the Provincial Marine from the lakes. Two hundred miles to the southeast, they had organized a rushed naval dockyard at the sleepy Pennsylvania town of Erie. Here, protected by a natural sandbar, the Americans were laying the keels of a new fleet of specially designed war vessels that could match the British in firepower and beat them for command of the water.

After the fall of Detroit, dockyards were in short supply on the American side of Lake Erie. Lieutenant Jesse Elliot, for the moment the overall American commander on the lake, placed his headquarters at Black Rock, two miles from Buffalo and the site of a small prewar naval dockyard. The establishment at Black Rock lay on the American side of the mouth of the Niagara River, and its position was dangerously exposed to the guns of the British Fort Erie on the Canadian side. From time to time, workers were scattered by British round shot, and convincing them to return to work under these circumstances became more and more of an issue for Elliot. Building the vessels necessary to fight the British for supremacy over the lakes became an increasingly challenging, and it was evident that a secondary location for construction was needed.

Thus Erie, a small harbour town whose peacetime economy depended on the Great Lakes salt trade, became the American head-quarters for warship building on the upper lakes. Although officially a town, Erie's motley collection of houses stretched over less than a square mile of ground hacked from the virgin Lake Erie shoreline. While in dry weather it could be reached by road from Pittsburgh and Buffalo, it was mostly accessible only by water; in particular, goods and supplies could be shipped only over Lake Erie or a collection of streams and rivers from Pittsburgh.

But while geography had made Erie inconvenient as a supply desti-nation, it had also made the town a perfect marshalling place of naval lake power. Around Erie Harbor stretched the long, protective arm of the Presque Isle peninsula. Reaching almost completely from west to east, the sandy peninsula was open only at the eastern end, where a narrow, shifting channel featured a dangerously shallow sandbar. This sandbar acted as a natural barrier against all but the smallest boats, and meant that work on an American lake fleet could proceed unmolested at Erie.

Erie could also count Daniel Dobbins among its assets. Dobbins was an experienced lake captain who before the war had run a fur-supply boat, the *Salina*, out of Erie itself. After witnessing the American humiliation at Michilimackinac first-hand, Dobbins was called to Washington to give a full report to the cabinet on the situation on the Upper Lakes. In September 1812 he was ordered to begin construction on four gunboats at Erie. Although Dobbins had no shipbuilding experience, he quickly rounded up the necessary labourers and supplies and brought in a shipwright, Ebenezer Crosby, from New York state. That autumn, work began on the first of the four gunboats, and even though Dobbins exhausted his budget before Christmas, the Lake Erie fleet was taking shape under his watchful eye.[66]

Finances were not Dobbins's only problem. Most of the American naval supplies were being diverted to Sackets Harbor, the naval yard near the eastern end Lake Ontario. Like the British, the Americans viewed the lowest of the Great Lakes as being the key to controlling the rest. All British supplies, troops and other war materiel had to come down the St. Lawrence and up Lake Ontario to reach the west, or else follow a twisting and difficult northern route up the Ottawa and French rivers and out onto Georgian Bay and Lake Huron. The American plan called for mastery of Lake Ontario in order to cut the British line of supply at its source, thus forcing the British either to maintain their western bases through the Ottawa River route or to abandon Upper Canada and the western fur-trading posts all together.

The flaw in the Americans' plan was that the British already knew of their geographic weakness and were prepared to do what was necessary to maintain their water routes. The British quickly amassed a fleet on Lake Ontario and set about to build more vessels at the Kingston shipyards. The American commander at Sackets Harbor was therefore engaged in a naval arms race with his British counterparts just across the lake. The strategic importance of Lake Ontario for both sides meant that fleet construction on Lake Erie could take second place, and thus the Provincial Marine at Amherstburg encountered many of the same problems getting necessary supplies and sailors as did the Americans at Black Rock and Erie.

The importance of Lake Ontario was such that Commodore Isaac Chauncey, the overall American commander on the lakes (and based at

Sackets Harbor) only visited the Erie yard once. He and his master ship designer, Henry Eckford, arrived in November 1812 and decided that the gunboats Dobbins and his makeshift crew were constructing were too small for lake service. Construction had advanced so quickly, though, that two of the boats had to be left as they were; the remaining two were modified to the new specifications. With the exception of this one visit, and a solitary discouraging letter from Elliot, Dobbins had no other contact with his superior officers and was left to scrounge up what materials he could on his own.[67]

Naval supplies were not the only problem for the soldiers in the Northwest. With primitive infrastructure on both the American and British sides of Lake Erie, amassing enough food to keep the armies fed became an increasing problem. Before the war, Great Lakes captains such as Mackintosh and Dobbins had made a living by transporting supplies to the isolated posts around the lakes. Now, with thousands of extra soldiers to feed, both sides were becoming aware of the limited resources of the area.

On 26 February 1813, while the *Nancy* lay snuggled in winter quarters, a worried, far-thinking Alexander Mackintosh, his brother Duncan, father Angus, and forty-four other prominent residents of Sandwich presented a memorandum to Prevost, warning him of several unique aspects of warfare in the Northwest, including the traditional tactics of the Natives, the close proximity of a growing American army, and of the clear and present danger of a food shortage for 1813. "The Militia of the District having been kept absent from their Agricultural concerns, a very large proportion of the last years crops were destroyed, and that very little wheat was sown last fall, which will produce a great scarcity during the ensuing season." The memorandum explained "That this evil can alone be palliated by suffering the Inhabitants to remain as much as possible on their Farms, and raising spring crops of Indian corn, oats, etc."[68] In a prescient recommendation, the inhabitants asked for more regular troops to take the burden of combat off the militia, so they could tend to their crops and feed the army. It is unknown whether Prevost ever received the memorandum or, if he did, whether he thought the inhabitants were serious in their warnings or simply trying to escape militia duty. Regardless, that March Procter was reinforced with two

In 1812, Brigadier General William Henry Harrison was the governor of Indiana Territory and an experienced military leader. Following Hull's surrender at Detroit, Harrison rebuilt and led the U.S. army of the Northwest. After constructing a strong base at Fort Meigs, on the Miami River, Harrison took advantage of the American victory on Lake Erie and give chase to the retreating British army. He caught and defeated the British at the battle of Moraviantown on 5 October 1813. The action resulted in the death of Tecumseh and the loss of Detroit and Amherstburg to the British. In 1841 Harrison was elected President of the United States, but died after only one month in office. ("General William Henry Harrison," artist Charles William Jefferys / Library and Archives Canada / C-73587)

more companies of the 41st — and with even more mouths to feed, the spectre of the supply crisis loomed as the winter thawed into spring.[69]

On the American side, as the shipbuilders busied themselves in the wilderness around Erie, building the fleet to sweep the British from the freshwater seas, the American Army of the Northwest was reconstituting itself. Command was given over to General William Henry Harrison, the tough governor of Indiana and the architect of many American offensives against the borderland Native tribes. Harrison's Indiana Territory had been fighting an on-again, off-again war with the Native groups for close to a decade, and his Indiana militia had played a major role in the Battle of Tippecanoe. Harrison was dedicated to the cause of securing the Northwest for the United States, and to eliminating any opposition from either the British or the Natives.

Harrison had begun to collect his forces at Fort Wayne during the summer of 1812. Fort Wayne was at the nexus of several major rivers, and was nearly halfway between the western tip of Lake Erie and the southern tip of Lake Michigan. Its central position was ideal for Harrison to carry out the expeditionary style of warfare he had perfected as governor of Indiana.[70] Harrison initially planned to attack the western extremity of Upper Canada again that autumn, but the threat of protracted frontier warfare with the Native nations, as well as logistical problems, forced him to abandon his fall campaign. Instead, he marshalled his forces and prepared for winter combat. He constructed a string of forts to protect his supply routes and moved one wing of his army to the Miami rapids, a strategic location on the old Detroit road and only fifty miles from Amherstburg. Bad weather and impassable terrain made the buildup of supplies nearly impossible. Despite the efforts of the women of Ohio to stitch heavy shirts for the frontier troops, Harrison's men remained freezing and sick. By Christmas, Harrison began to doubt he could make any kind of advance toward Canada before the spring.[71]

In January 1813 a group of Kentucky militia were sent north to the small settlement of Frenchtown. The village, on the banks of the Raisin River, was just to the north of the Miami River and a major depot along the Detroit road. The British and Native allies had been requisitioning corn from Frenchtown, and American militia commanders believed they should take the town to protect the American supporters there.

When the Kentucky militia approached Frenchtown on 18 January, two companies of the Essex militia, several hundred Potowatami and Wyandot warriors, and a single howitzer engaged them. The Americans advanced across the frozen river under heavy fire and eventually pushed the militia and Natives back into the woods. With the Americans in possession of the town, both sides called for reinforcements. American General James Winchester arrived in Frenchtown and set up camp. Four days later, on 22 January, General Procter himself arrived with a mixed force of regular soldiers, including detachments from the 41st and Royal Newfoundland Regiments, as well as the Essex militia, Native warriors, artillerymen and twenty-eight men from the Provincial Marine whose vessels were laid up for the winter.[72]

It was a hard-fought engagement. Procter brought his men to the edge of the same woods that the Essex militia and Pottowatomies had escaped through just days before. He concentrated his artillery and regulars in the middle, with Natives on his right wing and the militia, backed up by more Natives, on his left. The Americans had neglected to post sentries, and as dawn broke the sight of long lines of British soldiers surprised them. The American regulars hastily formed up in the open while the Kentucky militia posted themselves behind a line of picket fencing on the edge of the village.[73]

Procter opened fire with his artillery and ordered his regulars forward. The redcoats advanced across open fields as the cannon shot smashed into the exposed American regulars. Natives on the British left circled around and began firing into the flank of the American regulars. For about twenty minutes the intense gunfire ripped into the American regulars. They wavered, and then broke and fled across the Raisin River.[74] With the regulars gone, the Kentucky militia was alone. Procter ordered his regulars to make several frontal assaults on the protected militia position, but the Kentuckians fought hard. The British redcoats' charges were beaten off, and they suffered heavy casualties. The British advanced their guns, but placed them out in the open where they were quickly picked off by keen-eyed American riflemen. The intense fighting could not last long, however. The American militia eventually began to run out of ammunition, and when a group of Natives captured General Winchester along with some of the retreating regulars, the American militia decided they had had enough. The militia surrendered at eleven o'clock in the morning.[75]

When the smoke cleared, Procter had taken the town and captured several hundred Americans. His force had also sustained heavy casualties. The British losses numbered 24 killed and more than 150 wounded. The 41st Regiment, the Royal Newfoundland Regiment and the Marine Department suffered the vast majority of the casualties.[76] The Marine Department sailors had been working the exposed artillery, while it had fallen to the regulars to mount the frontal assaults on the militia position. The Americans had also suffered greatly. Over 500 American troops were taken prisoner, and while accurate casualty lists are unavailable, certainly close to 300 were killed and wounded.[77] Afraid that a larger American force was on its way to Frenchtown, Procter collected his troops and prisoners and retreated back to Detroit.

Harrison was not on his way to Frenchtown, but Procter's hasty withdrawal left many seriously wounded American prisoners unattended in the village. On the night of 22 January and in the morning of the 23rd, several of these prisoners were killed by a small group of straggling Native warriors. What became known as the massacre of the River Raisin became an American rallying cry against the British for the rest of the war.[78]

The result of the Battle of Frenchtown was to delay any further movement by Harrison. Convinced of the superiority of the British force, and wary of another attack cutting his lines of communications, Harrison himself retreated to the Sandusky River to the southeast.[79] After some hesitation, Harrison returned to rapids on the Miami River and began construction of a new strongpoint. Named Fort Meigs, it was the obvious springboard to the invasion of Michigan and Upper Canada.

Throughout the same winter, preparations for the Lake Erie fleet continued. Dobbins and his men worked unceasingly, and in March 1813 Commodore Oliver Hazard Perry and a new shipwright, Noah Brown, arrived at Erie. Perry had been ordered to take command of the growing flotilla, and while Dobbins remained the foreman, Perry scoured the Pennsylvania countryside for the necessary materials, armaments and supplies.

From
Portrait by
Jarvis, in
City Hall New York

Sent to Lake Erie in the winter of 1812-1813, professional U.S. naval officer Captain Oliver Hazard Perry accelerated the American shipbuilding activities at Erie, Pennsylvania. Perry's fleet of newly constructed warships took to the open lake in the summer of 1813, and on 10 September 1813 he defeated the British Lake Erie squadron at the Battle of Put-in-Bay. Following his victory, however, Perry fell into conflict with his subordinate, Lieutenant Jesse Elliot, and requested to be transferred. For his defeat of the Royal Navy on Lake Erie, Perry became an American hero. ("Captain Oliver Hazard Perry," artist Charles William Jefferys / Library and Archives Canada / C-73586)

American strategists worked out a new plan for the invasion of Canada. Isaac Chauncey was to direct his efforts against Kingston, cutting off Upper Canada from Lower Canada and strangling the isolated garrisons along the Detroit and Niagara frontiers. In the spring of 1813, however, the American senior commanders, Commodore Issac Chauncey and Major General Henry Dearborn, got cold feet. They received intelligence that Kingston had been heavily reinforced by the British and they began to doubt their ability to take the vital naval base. Chauncey and Dearborn explained to the Secretary of the Navy that they were afraid the British would be able to defend Kingston long enough to make any follow-up operations impossible. Instead, Chauncey suggested a sweeping revision to the American plan of attack. Reviving the old thoughts about attacks on multiple fronts, Chauncey suggested that he first land a force at York to destroy the British naval ships in the harbour. With command of the lake, he could then support an American offensive along the Niagara River. Similarly, by capturing Fort Erie, the Americans could finally release the boats Elliot's men had been preparing at Black Rock. Combining these with the boats that Dobbins had been building at Erie would give the Americans sufficient advantage that they could destroy the British Lake Erie fleet, recapture Detroit, and then move on to Lake Huron and retake Michilimackinac.

"This would give us such a decided advantage in the upper province and such an influence over the Indians," Chauncey concluded, "that I think the Enemy would abandon the upper country altogether and concentrate his forces about Kingston and Montreal. In that event it would leave us at liberty to bring nearly the whole of our force (naval as well as military) to act upon any one point."[80] Chauncey's sweeping revisions to the American battle plans were approved,[81] and he and Dearborn set about coordinating the details.

As a result of the new plan, the responsibilities of the Erie dockyards increased. In preparation for the new offensive, two more vessels were ordered to be constructed under the shelter of Presque Isle. These were to be larger than the gunboats Erie had been previously assigned to build. They were to be brigs — larger ships with two masts and decks designed to hold twenty guns apiece. While the Provincial Marine was using converted peacetime cargo sloops like the *Nancy*, the United States Navy was building vessels especially designed for war.

The British knew nothing of the overall American battle plans, but as the ice began to break up, it became eminently clear that Procter had to act again or would risk being overwhelmed by Harrison's growing army. The battle of Frenchtown in January had bought him some months as Harrison reorganized and reconstructed the American Army of the Northwest. With the ice clearing from the lake, the British could also bring the Provincial Marine out of winter quarters and once again begin their domination of the lakes. Controlling the water meant quick movement, plenty of supplies, and the ability to transport artillery without having to contend with the rough roads and washouts of the Black Swamp wilderness.

The British fleet was needed to support Procter's efforts in the west. Supplies had to be run from Fort Erie to Amherstburg and Detroit. More importantly, it would give Procter the ability to make offensive strikes against the Americans. As the *Nancy* glided from the Detroit River into the cold waters of Lake Erie, she and her sisters of the Provincial Marine were put almost immediately back to work against the Army of the Northwest.

Procter planned an expedition directly against Harrison's strongpoint on the rapids. Fort Meigs was to be attacked by an amphibious combined force of regulars, militia and Natives, supported by the Provincial Marine. The *Nancy*, along with the Provincial Marine vessels *Lady Prevost* and *General Hunter*, and with the hired transports *Chippewa*, *Mary* and *Miamis*, left Amherstburg on 23 April. Accompanying them were two gunboats and enough bateaux to carry over 400 militiamen. The decks of the *Nancy* alone were crammed with ninety British soldiers, including fifty-six members of the Royal Newfoundland Regiment, twenty-eight members of the Royal Artillery, and members of Commissariat General's office. The other transports carried the bulk of the 41st Regiment, the general's staff and five members of the 10th Royal Veterans Battalion.[82] Tecumseh and 1,200 Native warriors travelled overland.

The *Nancy* and the rest of Procter's flotilla arrived at the mouth of the Miami River on 28 April. The British troops solemnly disembarked from the lake schooners as Tecumseh's warriors filled the woods on both sides of the river. Two gunboats, *Eliza* and *Myers*, crept upstream with the siege artillery.

Fort Meigs was an imposing military target. Constructed under the supervision of Captain Eleazer Wood, a West Point–trained military engineer, the fort sat on top of a commanding elevation next to the Miami River. The fort was protected by a deep ravine to the south and by a creek to the east. The wooden walls were reinforced with mounds of thick earth and were pierced with several batteries of guns with interlocking fields of fire. It was surrounded by an abatis, a rough fence made from felled trees that could easily stop an infantry assault. Inside, the fort contained strong blockhouses and military storehouses. As Procter's men filed through the woods, the American troops also hastily built traverses, long mounds of earth designed to prevent cannon shot from bouncing around inside the fort.[83]

As Procter's men set about building the first siege batteries across the Miami River, it began to rain. For five days the rain drenched the tough soldiers dragging the guns into position. The massive twenty-four-pounder guns had to be hauled to the battery sites by scores of men and teams of oxen. Gun carriages sank axle-deep in the drenching downpour, and intermittent bombardments from Fort Meigs slowed the work. On 1 May the batteries were finally completed, and Procter's artillery opened fire.[84]

For four days the artillery kept up a constant barrage. Procter added a new battery, with five-and-a-half- and eight-and-a-half-inch mortars, to the south bank of the Miami River. The soft mud helped to absorb the impact of much of the British fire. The mortar shells buried themselves in the soft earth, and their fuses were extinguished in the damp muck. The traverses inside the fort stopped the heaviest British shot from doing any great damage to the American troops. But it was the buildings inside the fort that most attracted the British gunners' attention. The roofs of the storehouses and blockhouses were all shot away.[85]

As the *Nancy* waited anxiously at the mouth of the river, Procter's pre-emptive strike was running into difficulties. The American engineers had built Fort Meigs well, giving it a commanding position on the south bank of the river and strong defensive works that frustrated the British gunners. By 5 May they had hardly dented the American fortress

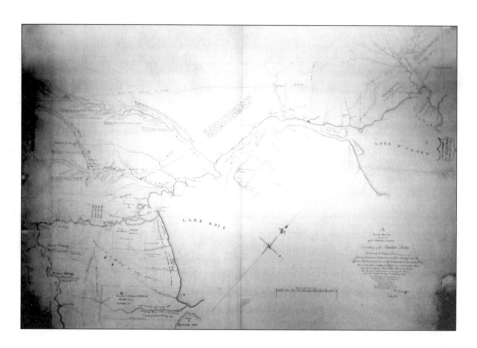

This map is of the western end of Lake Erie, showing the Detroit River and the Miami River. In 1813 Major General Henry Procter led two failed expeditions to the American Fort Meigs, located on the Miami River. The *Nancy* acted as a transport and supply ship on both expeditions. In both cases she anchored in the mouth of the Miami River, and sent boats to land supplies and troops. ("Rough Sketch of part of Wayne County Territory of United States North-West of River Ohio..." by Robert King after Patrick McNiff / National Archives and Records Administration, College Park, Maryland / RG 77, Records of the Chief of Engineers, Civil Works, US 119.)

when a sudden reinforcement of Kentucky militia swept up both sides of the river. The attack surprised the British besiegers, who for a time lost control of their batteries. The British quickly recovered, however, and a counterattack by the 41st Regiment destroyed the American force. Nearly five hundred American prisoners were marched off the field, while more were taken privately by Procter's Native allies.[86]

Despite his success on 5 May, Procter's attack on Fort Meigs was quickly winding down. Conditions in the British camp were miserable: tents were scarce, and the rain-soaked soldiers tried everything to stay dry. "A few slips of bark torn from the surrounding trees, and covering the skeleton of a hut, was their only habitation," recalled one British soldier after the war. "Hence arose dysentery, ague, and the various other ills to which an army, encamped in a wet and unhealthy position is invariably subject."[87] The squalid camp conditions increased the misery of the troops, particularly the non-professional militia. They began to slowly desert as the siege entered its second week.

The militia also had worries beyond mud and rain: they were worried about their crops. The fighting the previous autumn had disrupted the normal cycle of planting and harvesting, and as the siege entered its tenth day the thoughts of the militiamen turned to the health of their food supply. On 6 May, all the company commanders from the Kent and Essex militia signed a petition to Procter explaining that if their men did not go home soon, the summer wheat and corn crops would be lost, "and that the consequence must be a famine next winter."[88] Based at the very end of the British supply line, and with an army that was already consuming more than the local population could supply, Procter could not afford to lose the season's produce. While the American attack failed to dislodge the British, Procter was forced to pull out shortly afterward because his force was rapidly dwindling.

Siege warfare required patience and an understanding of the logic of attrition. The militia possessed neither, and was soon melting home. Procter also reported that the Native warriors were losing patience with the siege. "I also received a Deputation of Indian Chiefs," Procter reported to Prevost, "counseling me to return, as they could not prevent their People, as was their Custom after any Battle of consequence, returning to their Villages, with their Wounded, their Prisoners and

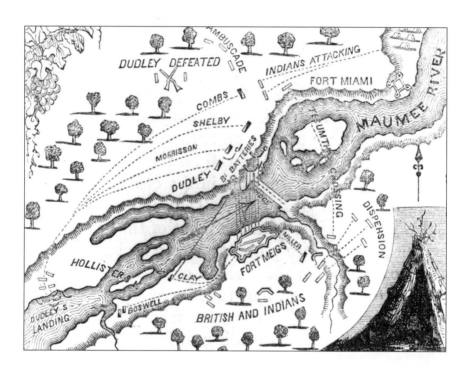

U.S. Army Engineers constructed Fort Meigs in the winter of 1812–1813. Located on the Miami River, not far from Lake Erie, Fort Meigs acted as a supply and staging base for the American army of the Northwest. Designed to be a strong defensive work, Fort Meigs withstood two sieges by British forces in spring and summer of 1813, and served as a springboard for Harrison's advance into Upper Canada in the fall of 1813. This map shows the troop movements during the American sortie against the British positions during the first siege of Fort Meigs on 5 May 1813. ("Siege of Fort Meigs," from B.J. Lossing, *The Pictorial Field-Book of the War of 1812*, New York, 1869 / Library and Archives Canada / C-010740)

Plunder, of which they had taken a considerable Quantity in the Boats of the Enemy."[89] Without enough regular troops to continue the siege, Procter was forced to pack his force back on its boats. The *Nancy* and the other vessels were obliged to re-embark the troops and point their bows back toward Amerherstburg.

The end of the siege gave Harrison some breathing room. His strongpoint at the southern end of the Detroit road was saved, although once again Procter's attack had cost him time. But time was now on Harrison's side. In the east, Chauncey had built a new fleet at Sackets Harbor and had acted on his battle plan.

At eight o'clock on the morning on 27 April, seventeen hundred United States troops disembarked from Commodore Chauncey's squadron a mile from the Upper Canadian shore. Chauncey had drawn his ships in as close to the shore as he could, and selected a landing place just to the west of the entrance to the harbour and not far from the town itself. The American seamen rowed hard for the shore, and soon an advance detachment of American riflemen "landed under a heavy fire from Indians & other troops."[90]

The British forces were small but prepared to resist fiercely. They had seen Chauncey's fleet drawing closer the day before, and Major General Roger Sheaffe had already called out the militia and his small garrison. Sheaffe's problem was that he did not know where the Americans would land, and so the previous night he had been forced to spread his small garrison on all sides of the town to prevent the British from being surprised. As Chauncey's boats struck for the Canadian shore, however, the American move was obvious and Sheaffe could direct his forces. Detachments of British regulars and militia were called in from the east side of town, and Major Givens and some Native warriors were sent to oppose the landing. Givens and the Natives arrived in time to meet the American riflemen as they jumped from their boats, and poured out a deadly fire as the Americans tried to organize themselves on the beach.[91]

Despite the resistance from the Natives, the Americans gained a foothold on Upper Canadian soil and pushed Givens and his men out of the way. When the British regulars arrived on the scene, the grenadier company of the 8th Regiment made a heroic charge on the beach and drove the Americans back to their boats. American numbers soon told, however, and slowly the British were pushed back to a defensive gun emplacement called the Western Battery.[92]

The Western Battery was an earth-and-stone fortification armed with cannon and designed to defend York's harbour against enemy shipping. As the Americans advanced on the town, their ships kept up a constant fire on the Western Battery. During the heated bombardment the Western Battery's magazine exploded with massive force. Deadly shards and clumps of earth rained down on Americans and British alike. Soldiers on both sides lost their lives, and the American commander, General Zebulon Pike, was killed.[93] The American advance temporarily halted, but as the British tried to put their shattered defences in order it became apparent that the Americans were simply too numerous.

Sheaffe first ordered his men back to York, then marched them quickly out of town down the Kingston road. York fell into American hands. The Americans immediately burned the provincial parliament buildings and the military storehouses. They also destroyed the skeleton of the *Isaac Brock,* a thirty-gun ship that was to have been built for the Provincial Marine. The Americans also captured the *General Hunter*, which they burned, and the *Duke of Gloucester*, which they later discovered was unfit for service.[94] Fortunately for the British, the *Prince Regent*, which had been in York that winter, had left a few days before the arrival of Chauncey's fleet.

The Americans remained at York only a short while. On 8 May, thinking that the British would be sufficiently disturbed by the capture of the provincial capital, Chauncey re-embarked the troops and headed for Fort Niagara. The American strategy for 1813 was proceeding as planned.

A month later, American armies captured Forts George and Erie along the Niagara River, cutting the most direct supply route to Procter's isolated western command. As the Americans marched toward Burlington, events on Lake Ontario seemed perilous and every effort was made to gain superiority there. Royal Navy sailors, officers and supplies from Nova Scotia and New Brunswick were funnelled to Kingston and only trickled west. Procter's shortage of everything from regular troops to flour continued, and Prevost could only spare him what little could be pared off from the Niagara area.

Meanwhile, Perry and Dobbins continued their work at Erie. On 19 June, Perry was able to report to the Secretary of the Navy that he had succeeded in bringing Elliot's boats from Black Rock. The finishing touches were being put on the rigging and armament of the brigs, and the gunboats were only waiting for additional ammunition. Elliot's boats, "although not well fitted, are considered as ready for service at a moment's notice."[95] All he needed to bring the boats over the protective sandbar were additional reinforcements of sailors.

The British were aware of the situation and were trying to make up for lost time in rectifying it. The Royal Navy official assumed responsibility for the Provincial Marine on 22 April. From then on, professional and battle-hardened seamen from the Atlantic were sent up the St. Lawrence to build and man the British vessels on the inland seas. The bones of a new ship, *Detroit*, were taking shape at Amherstburg. A new commander, Captain Robert Heriot Barclay, arrived on Lake Erie in May. He was possessed of undaunted courage and undiminished dedication, all in the Nelsonian mould. Barclay was a career naval officer. He entered the Royal Navy at age twelve, and by eighteen he was a serving lieutenant. He had been in numerous engagements and battles against the French, including the battle of Trafalgar in 1805. In 1807 he lost his arm attacking a French convoy, and was later ordered to North America. In March 1813, after serving in several frigates sailing out of Halifax, an action-hardened Barclay was ordered to the freshwater battle-fields. He took command at Kingston, but was replaced two months later when a more senior officer, Sir James Yeo, arrived on Lake Ontario with more reinforcements. Yeo was placed in overall command, and after another captain turned down the Lake Erie command, Barclay was posted to Amherstburg as fleet commodore.[96]

One of Barclay's priorities as commander on Lake Erie was to keep an eye on the rapidly progressing American fleet at Erie. Procter desperately wanted to launch a pre-emptive strike against the dockyards thereby eliminating the threat that Perry's wilderness fleet posed to the Right Division. But the British failed to move. The natural defensive sandbar across Erie Harbor made it impossible for the Provincial Marine to act proactively, and Procter hesitated at the idea of attacking the post without a significant reinforcement of regular troops.[97] Instead of mounting

In the spring of 1813 Commodore Sir James Lucas Yeo took command of the Royal Navy on the Great Lakes. Yeo ordered young Lieutenant Miller Worsley to take command of the *Nancy* and other British naval forces on Lake Huron in the summer of 1814. Based at Kingston, Upper Canada, Yeo oversaw the massive British shipbuilding effort on the Great Lakes. ("Sir James L. Yeo," artist Charles William Jefferys / Library and Archives Canada / C-70393)

a pre-emptive strike at the growing American fleet, all Barclay could do was keep an eye on the rapid progress behind Presque Isle and report it back to Procter.

Nonetheless, Barclay's arrival took some of the weight off Procter's shoulders. "I am confident of the most cordial Cooperation and Aid from Captain Barclay whose Arrival lessened considerably my Anxiety." But the pressures of being at the end of an extended line of supply and communication were still heavy. Procter was short of everything, from troops to supplies to money. "The Service in this District has been much impeded by the total want of military Artificers. I have Reason to apprehend, an Intention of detaining in the other District a Portion of the 41st Regt: whom they have found useful as Artificers and other, which if so, I heartily hope will not be sanctioned. We have scarcely the Means of constructing even a Blockhouse." He complained to Prevost, "It is incumbent on me to acquaint Your Excellency that the Service has been much impeded by the very scanty and irregular Supplies of money which have been received by the Commissariat in this District."[98] By the end of June, he had run out of ammunition and guns to arm his Native allies. Worse, his food supplies had run so low that Native warriors and their families were eating bread alone. The area around Amherstburg had been so denuded of supplies that a herd of seventy-two cattle were sent by the commander of the Centre Division to help relieve Procter's food situation.[99]

Despite the added meat supply, Procter's situation steadily deteriorated as the spring turned into fall. "I resolved, notwithstanding the Smallness of that Force to move, and where we might be fed at the Expense of the Enemy."[100] Once again the *Nancy* and the other vessels were crammed with fighting men, and at the end of July the little navy set sail once again for the Miami River.

On 19 July, Procter and his flotilla set sail for Fort Meigs for the second time. After a journey of three days, the *Nancy* discharged her cargo, anchored in the mouth of the Miami River and waited as the action took place out of sight, beyond the wooded riverbanks. Procter's force managed to ascend the Miami River without being noticed. The Americans inside the fort knew nothing of Procter's movement until the morning of 21 July, when some of Tecumseh's Natives ambushed a party

Commodore Robert Barclay took command of the British Lake Erie squadron after Yeo's arrival in Upper Canada. A battle-scarred veteran, Barclay had fought in the Battle of Trafalgar in 1805 and had lost his left arm in another action in 1809. From his base in Amherstburg, Barclay strove to contain the American squadron at Erie, Pennsylvania, and worked under difficult conditions to improve and augment his fleet. Barclay was severely wounded during the British defeat at the Battle of Put-in-Bay. His actions in the battle earned him the deep respect of his American opponents. ("Captain Robert Barclay," artist Charles William Jefferys / Library and Archives Canada / C-70396)

of Americans leaving the fort.[101] The Americans, led by General Green Clay, quickly rushed to arms and prepared themselves for another siege. Procter set about building batteries again, but his heavy guns had been placed aboard the Royal Navy vessels that were currently blockading the American flotilla at Erie. All Procter could mount against Fort Meigs was a couple of small six-pounders. Rather than battering down the walls of Fort Meigs, Procter would have to try another tactic.

The inspiration, perhaps, came on 23 July. General Green Clay had become puzzled as to why the British had not opened fire with heavy artillery, as they had in April. He sent a small scouting party outside the fort to observe the British preparations, and it was promptly ambushed by some Natives. The scouting party rushed back to Fort Meigs unscathed, but the episode seemed to have given Tecumseh an idea.[102]

The veteran Native leader suggested that since the British could not get inside the fort, they should draw the Americans outside. He proposed that a body of Natives move through the woods and out of sight along the path to Sandusky. The warriors would then stage a mock battle, firing their weapons in the air and making all the noises and sounds of a real skirmish. The Americans inside the fort would think that General Harrison was marching to their rescue and had engaged the British forces down the road. The Americans would then rush from their fort to the aid of their fictitious comrades. Once the American troops had left the fort, the British would attack their rear, storm the open front gates, and capture the fort.[103] With no other ideas of his own, Procter accepted Tecumseh's plan.

On the evening of 26 July, Tecumseh swung into action. The British lay in wait as the Natives began their mock battle. As the shots and shouts of the Natives thundered out of the wilderness, Clay and the other Americans in the fort were unimpressed. "This evening they gave us a sham battle amongst themselves along the trace and nearly in view; not doubt to decoy us out."[104] No Americans rushed out of the fort. The gates remained closed, and the garrison remained safe inside. Eventually the Natives and British became discouraged, and the mock battle ended.

Meanwhile, with his vessel loaded with provisions and artillery for the British force, Mackintosh and his crew had to keep the *Nancy* close to the action. On 25 July, a curious and daring Mackintosh had "sent the men for wood. I go up to Headquarters & from there within gunshot of the American Fort."[105] There, the scene was much as it had been in April. The British regulars had taken up a position opposite Fort Meigs, while the Natives took up encircling positions in the surrounding woods. Unlike the first siege, however, this time Procter did not have any heavy guns with which to batter the ramparts of Fort Meigs.[106] Mackintosh idled around the British camp and watched as more supply boats from Amherstburg and the Raisin River came down to the British positions. As it became apparent that the small British cannon could not dent the thick walls of the American fort, rumour circulated that they would soon be moving to the Sandusky River, in Ohio. Fort Stephenson, just up the Sandusky River, was on one of Harrison's supply routes to the Ohio interior. Attacking the fort would again interrupt Harrison's buildup, and any captured provisions would help feed the British army.

Rumours swirled, but nothing happened. Mackintosh returned to the *Nancy* and oversaw the unloading of more ammunition. In the afternoon came on a violent thunderstorm. Lightning crackled through the sky and Mackintosh was kept busy tending to the *Nancy* as she bobbed in the heavy westerly swells and was pelted by rain. The troops on shore were soaked as well, as the Americans sat comfortably behind their walls. Later that day, men of the *Nancy* found that their cooking pan had been pilfered by the crew of the *Ellen*, a hired transport about half the size of the *Nancy*. The *Ellen*, captained by a man named Miller, was owned by Richard Pattinson and was a rival of the *Nancy*'s in the Great Lakes shipping trade. As the campaign, and the summer of 1813, wore on, relations between crew of the two vessels became strained as the crews took turns purloining small items from one another.

The 26th of July found the *Nancy*'s crew busy splicing a broken hawser and making wadding for the British guns. Even though they were well out in the mouth of the river, they could still hear the crackle of gunfire and rumble of guns from the direction of the fort. Later rumours brought them stories of skirmishes between the Natives and a band of Americans. The Americans were trying to carry letters into Fort Meigs when they were attacked, the story went, and only escaped because they threw away their packages.[107]

Without enough firepower to reduce any of the walls of Fort Meigs, Procter found himself in an awkward position. The fort was too strong to storm by frontal assault and, as in April, the Native warriors were becoming restless. The Americans were content to stay behind their strong walls, and after a couple of days the troops became restless and the Natives began to trickle home. Procter was forced to move on to a different target, or else face the withering away of his army.

Those rumours Mackintosh had heard the first day at Fort Meigs proved ultimately to be correct. Procter ordered the troops back to the ships to reload them and set sail for Fort Stephenson. On the morning of 28 July the *Nancy* and the other vessels weighed anchor and headed east, toward the Sandusky River, while Tecumseh's Natives made their way overland toward the small American post.

Fort Stephenson was a tiny encampment in the wilderness, fifty miles up the river. Procter expected there to be an abundance of cattle nearby, which he hoped he could use to feed his hungry Native allies and help alleviate some of his own supply problems. Procter planned to attack the fort and quickly overwhelm the defenders, giving his men time to collect what available provisions there were and then leave before American reinforcements could arrive from the neighbouring areas.[108]

At five in the morning of 31 July, the *Nancy* and the rest of the convoy dropped anchor at the mouth of the Sandusky River. As passengers this time, Mackintosh had none other than General Procter and his staff, as well as several artillery pieces and some sheep for the British army. Mackintosh and the rest of the crew spent most of that afternoon and evening unloading the small six-pound pieces of artillery Procter planned to use against the fort. Procter at this point seems to have lost his self-confidence. Mackintosh, eager for some idea as to what was expected of the *Nancy*, was disappointed in the vague instructions he received from the British general. "I several times applied to the Gen'l (previous to his departure) for instructions but could get no positive assurance from him, the only one was that I should wait in the 2 Six pounders which in the Gun boats should be sent off to me."[109] By eight that evening, Procter and the *Nancy*'s cargo were safely ashore, and a nervous, uncertain Mackintosh ordered his men to keep a close eye out for any strange lights or other vessels.

The night passed peacefully, however. The following day, after tasking some of his men to routine ship maintenance, Mackintosh went to explore the coastline first-hand. He walked the deeply forested shore and found some pieces of the wreckage of a vessel. After a time, he watched as another British transport, its rival the *Ellen* (with its thieving crew), sent supplies up the river. By three o'clock that afternoon, Mackintosh was back on board, and again the *Nancy*'s crew could hear the distant sound of gunfire.

While the British troops and Native warriors began the siege of Fort Stephenson, Mackintosh had another run-in with Miller, the captain of the *Ellen*. As Mackintosh described it afterward, he "sent a ps. [piece] of rope to Mr. Miller, commanding the *Ellen*, which had been taken by mistake from his vessel on the Monday night of our departure from Amherstburg. He refuses to receive it, at the same time accusing the Men who came out with him of having stolen it."[110] The confrontation — or rather gamesmanship — that passed between the crews of the *Nancy* and the *Ellen*, helped alleviate boredom on board the *Nancy*. While the army was busy concerning itself with the American fortification, the crews of the transport vessels had nothing to do but wait out in the lake.

The next day, 2 August, Mackintosh again went exploring along the shoreline, and "Discovered several fresh human tracks & a number of tracks of cattle."[111] Mackintosh returned to the *Nancy* and, still bored, he brought her for a look into another bay on the other side of the river. With nothing new to be seen there, the *Nancy* returned to the starting anchorage and brought some hay on board for the sheep. When that was done, Mackintosh began sounding the bay.

A treacherous, sweeping sandy shoal protected the mouth of the Sandusky River. With only three to six feet of water running across it, the shoal effectively closed the mouth of the river to the navigation of large ships. The shoal was such an impediment, in fact, that Mackintosh nicknamed the water behind it "Lake Sandusky." With the spare time he now had, Mackintosh set the *Nancy* to work sounding the shoal, plumbing the depth of the water in search of some place deep enough for a deep-draft vessel to pass. Eventually, the meticulous probing paid off. The crew found a passage twenty fathoms wide with a depth of four to five fathoms, deep enough for the largest lake vessels to pass through, near the south end of the shoal.

The British supply ship *Chippewa* had spent the last day and a half tacking against stiff winds up into the mouth of the Sandusky River. The *Chippewa* was carrying Colonel William Evans of the 41st Regiment, as well as several other officers and men badly needed by Procter's invasion force. Unaware of the dangerous shoal, the *Chippewa* gave a friendly salute to the *Nancy* and then sailed straight for the entrance of the river. Mackintosh jumped in the *Nancy*'s boat and pulled hard for the *Chippewa*. Alarmed by Mackintosh's frantic chase, the *Chippewa* hove to, and was relieved to have been diverted from crashing into the sandbar.

That afternoon, more sounds of gunfire came from upstream. Later, a boat emerged from the river, hungry for provisions for the army. The fort was stronger than Procter had imagined, and the attack was not going well. Mackintosh, out of sight of the fighting but within hearing range — and certainly within the range of rumour — grew nervous again. Amid the sheep, hay and other provisions for Procter's army, Mackintosh somehow found room for a piece of defensive ordnance. He creatively mounted a three-pounder field gun on the cramped deck of the little fur-trading vessel, and perhaps slept a little better the night of 2 August.[112]

The gunfire the crew of the *Nancy* had heard that afternoon marked the final British assault on Fort Stephenson. The position was indeed much more heavily fortified than Procter had imagined, with "Blockhouses connected by Picketing which they flank, and is calculated for a garrison of five or six hundred men."[113] Nevertheless, the agents from the Indian Department told Procter that unless he attacked immediately, the Natives would lose all respect for him. Procter caved and ordered an assault. For two hours the light British cannon rapped at the wooden palisades on the north side of Fort Stephenson, while members of the 41st Regiment formed up and prepared to storm the American position.

Inside the fort, twenty-one-year-old Major George Croghan of the 17th United States Infantry Regiment prepared to receive the assault with only 160 men and one 6-pound gun. Croghan stationed his men and light cannon exactly where Procter's men attacked. At 5 p.m. the men of the 41st and the Native warriors charged straight into a blizzard of grapeshot and musket fire.[114] The Natives dispersed, and the British sounded the retreat soon afterward. With ninety-six casualties and no means of renewing the assault, Procter re-embarked his army on the little flotilla of ships, including the *Nancy*, that were waiting outside the Sandusky sandbar. Dejected, but safe at last, his force reached Amherstburg five days later.[115]

The expedition had been a failure. Harrison's buildup was barely interrupted, and Procter had lost more regular troops than he thought he could afford. In his report to Prevost, Procter complained bitterly about the behaviour of the Natives and the inhabitants of Frenchtown. He begged for more British redcoats and supplies. Prevost, preoccupied with the American offensives along the Niagara and Chauncey's fleet on Lake Ontario, could spare but a few men. With Harrison in the south, Perry at Erie, and the supply lines across Lake Ontario in doubt, the British hold on the Northwest was growing ever more tenuous.

Even so, the British and the North West Company still occupied the Gibraltar of the Great Lakes, the fur-trade fortress of Michilimackinac. Keeping Mackinac supplied and defended would guarantee British influence over the Native allies of the Northwest and continue to pin down American resources on the extremities of the colonies rather than at decisive points. Despite the growing shortage of supplies, Procter well knew the importance of the little northern island to the defence of Canada. When the *Nancy* returned to Moy after the failure of the Sandusky River expedition, she was rehired for the task of resupplying Michilimackinac.

By 31 August, three weeks after her return from Ohio, the *Nancy* was ready to sail again. She was jammed with flour and other food-stuffs, all in barrels, so that she was drawing a deep seven feet, two inches.[116] She also had a few passengers with her: Captain Richard Bullock, of the 41st Regiment, along with his family, was being posted to Mackinac. Bullock was taking over from Captain Charles Roberts, the conqueror of the island, who had taken ill. With Procter still in command of the Michigan Territory, the garrison at Michilimackinac was small and well within the command responsibilities of someone of Bullock's rank. An independent command, especially one with the logistical and diplomatic demands of Michilimackinac, was nonetheless a feather in the young officer's cap.

At ten o'clock in the morning, the trusty *Nancy* set sail for Mackinac. The voyage up into Lake Huron lasted ten days, most of which was spent fighting the strong current of the St. Clair River. On 3 September, the slowly moving vessel encountered the Native chief Black Bird, who delivered the disturbing news that a flotilla of five American vessels had appeared off Amherstburg. Procter, he advised, was marshalling his forces there, but nothing else was known. The *Nancy* continued its mission to Michilimackinac.

*   *   *

The summer had been a busy one for Oliver Hazard Perry and Daniel Dobbins. Five other vessels from Black Rock joined the two brigs and three gunboats under construction in the Erie yard. With the capture of Fort Erie and the Niagara River by American forces, Elliot found himself free at last to complete his gunboats. He also converted five merchant vessels, including the captured *Caledonia*, into American warships. Hauling by brute force against the current of the Niagara River, Elliot's men had armed the vessels in Buffalo and set sail for Erie.[117]

Barclay, aware that the Americans were attempting to combine their new Lake Erie fleet, tried to intercept Elliot's flotilla. Just as Barclay sighted the Americans, a fog settled between the two fleets. The Royal Navy lost the Americans in the limited visibility, and Elliot's boats snuck over the shallow sandbar into the safe lee of Presque Isle. Perry now had ten boats at his disposal, and for the first time since the war began, the motley collection of British vessels was outnumbered.

Not only were the British ships outnumbered, but they were out-gunned. Dobbins had organized a massive train of ordnance to bring heavy cannon for the Lake Erie fleet.[118] Stubby, powerful carronades and long twelve-pounder guns were mounted on the new warships, giving the Americans a considerable advantage in firepower. Besides the two new heavily armed brigs, the Americans had also put the finishing touches on the gunboats Dobbins had started the previous year. They were sleek schooners, with the shallow draft necessary for close lake operations. They also brandished one or two long heavy guns, mounted on swivels so that they could have a maximum arc of fire over the railings and bulwarks of the vessel. They added a powerful long-range punch to the heavy carronade broadsides of the brigs. Altogether it was a heavy American naval armament.

For the moment, then, all Barclay could do was to try and blockade Erie and threaten the American fleet if it tried to cross the sandbar. It was at this point that the Americans would be at their most vulnerable, as the ships would have to be stripped of their guns to give them as shallow a draft as possible. Unarmed, they would be easy prey for Barclay and the Royal Navy. But once they were in the open water it would be a tight contest.

Barclay could not stand off Erie indefinitely. Lacking supplies of food and fresh water, Barclay took advantage of what he thought was the Americans' inability to bring their ships over Erie's protective sandbar. One day in August, the Americans awoke to find the Royal Navy nowhere in sight. Seizing the opportunity, they ran their ships to the sandbar, unloaded the guns, stores and ammunition, and pushed them into the open waters of Lake Erie. By the time Barclay had returned, Perry's fleet of warships was at sea — and on the prowl. Horror-stricken, Barclay realized his error and dashed back to Amherstburg to complete the *Detroit*.[119]

As the *Nancy* was putting into Michilimakinac with its valuable cargo of passengers and food, the British flotilla was putting into Amherstburg. As Mackintosh was unloading barrels of flour, Barclay was loading barrels of gunpowder. Barclay stripped cannon from the defences of Fort Malden and pulled men from the Royal Newfoundland Regiment to act as extra sailors and marines. By the end of the first week of September, the veteran of Trafalgar was setting sail for the ultimate showdown with Perry's wilderness fleet.

Aboard the *Nancy*

hile Robert Barclay rushed to put the finishing touches on the *Detroit*, Oliver Hazard Perry was receiving some welcome reinforcements. On 10 August, Jesse Elliot arrived from Black Rock with over a hundred officers and men to man the new American lake fleet.[120] Perry's new fleet went to seek out Barclay and take command of the lake. With the new American squadron out in the open water, Barclay had no option but to run into the harbour at Amherstburg and muster his forces.

Because the lake was in American hands, all British freight traffic along Lake Erie stopped. This included the vital supply runs that kept Procter's army fed, clothed and stocked with ammunition. Procter's anxiety grew in direct proportion to the longer the Americans controlled the water and the lower his food reserves became. Tecumseh's Native warriors, who kept themselves and their families fed from British supplies as well, began to grumble as their stomachs also became empty.

Prevost, visiting his troops along the Niagara frontier, leaned heavily on Barclay to get things moving. He ordered an extra Royal Navy officer and about fifty men to leave Kingston and reinforce the Lake Erie flotilla. He then wrote to Procter, insisting that "The experience obtained by Sir Jas. Yeo conduct toward a Fleet infinitely superior to the one under his command will satisfy Captn. Barclay that he has only to dare & the Enemy is discomfited."[121] With his honour and Procter's army on the line, it was clear that Barclay had to move quickly.

At Amherstburg, Barclay had gathered together what he could of the Royal Navy's Lake Erie squadron and was hurrying the last details of *Detroit*, whose ordnance had not arrived. Her cannon had either been siphoned off to arm Yeo's growing Lake Ontario fleet or were stuck somewhere along the long, muddy supply line. Finally, Barclay could wait no longer and he had cannon from Fort Malden manhandled and jammed into the *Detroit*'s decks.[122] The brig had a confusing mixture of guns, but at least she was armed.

Barclay was also seriously short of experienced sailors. The ability to calmly and efficiently handle a ship under battle conditions was key to success. It meant that a commander had manoeuvrability and tactical options, and not just a floating battery of artillery. Those sailors Prevost had ordered from Kingston still had not arrived by the first week in September, and Procter and Barclay could not wait. Instead of the experienced seamen that Perry had received, Barclay topped up his crews with men of the Royal Newfoundland Regiment and 41st Regiment of Foot.[123]

While the soldiers provided much-needed support as marines, and while the Newfoundlanders had been serving on and off in the Provincial Marine and Royal Navy vessels since the outbreak of war, they were not the trained, able sailors Barclay needed so badly. Nonetheless, with his mixed crew and mixed armament, Barclay sailed on 10 September to dare Oliver Hazard Perry.

Perry's fleet numbered nine vessels, the largest and most powerful were the brigs *Niagara* and *Lawrence*. Each had been built by Dobbins and his team at Erie, and was freshly, correctly armed and outfitted for war. Perry also had the captured North West Company schooner *Caledonia*, which Elliot had nicely renovated at Black Rock. Then there were six gunboats. Four of these, *Tigress*, *Scorpion*, *Porcupine* and *Ariel*, had been built at Erie and were brand new fighting vessels. Two more, *Trippe* and *Somers*, had been commercial vessels before the war and retrofitted at Black Rock.

The American fleet had the advantage in firepower over the British flotilla. Where the *Detroit*, *Queen Charlotte* and *General Hunter* carried a collection of long guns with longer range, they were in general smaller than the American armament. For instance, both *Lawrence* and *Niagara* carried two twelve-pound long guns, and a battery of eighteen heavy-hitting thirty-two-pound carronades. The *Queen Charlotte* mounted three twelve-pound long guns, and fourteen twenty-four-pound carronades. In all, the weight of the new American fleet's broadside could outclass the British squadron by 912 pounds to 494.[124]

The American gunboats also packed a powerful punch. *Scorpion*, as an example, carried one huge thirty-two-pound long gun and a shorter thirty-two-pound carronade. Both were mounted on pivots with a brass track, a rotating mount that allowed a wide arc of fire and maximized the flexibility of her considerable firepower. The gunboat's long cannon helped compensate for Perry's range deficiency. By having the *Ariel* and *Scorpion* out in front of the line, he allowed their shots to tell on the British fleet before his own short-range smashers could be brought to bear.

Perry's fleet bore down on the Royal Navy in a following, light wind. The British line had *Chippewa* — the little schooner that the *Nancy* had prevented from running onto the sandbar at Sandusky a month earlier — in the lead. *Detroit, General Hunter, Queen Charlotte* and *Lady Prevost* followed, with the *Little Belt* in the rear. The Americans had the gunboats *Scorpion* and *Ariel*, designated to engage *Detroit* and *Chippewa* with their long guns, in the van. The *Lawrence, Caledonia* and *Niagara*, the meat of Perry's squadron, were next, followed by the remaining four gunboats.[125]

At 11:45, the British opened fire. Barclay's longer guns had better range than Perry's stout little carronades, and *Lawrence* began to disintegrate as it plowed headfirst into the British broadsides. When he was in range, Perry brought his carronade broadside to bear and began pounding the *Detroit* — all the while taking heavy fire from the *Detroit* and *Queen Charlotte*. The *Ariel* and *Scorpion* compensated somewhat by raking the *Detroit* and *Queen Charlotte* with heavy shot.[126]

The battle became intense. Despite heavy casualties on both sides, the guns kept firing. The *Queen Charlotte* moved ahead and brought her carronades to bear on *Lawrence*. For two hours the two largest British ships battered *Lawrence* as the remainder of the American line struggled to catch up in the whisper of wind. The aftermost schooners broke out their oars and hauled furiously for the battle, while Elliot, in command of the second American brig *Niagara*, tried to maintain his position in the line of battle and still keep his long twelve-pounders firing.

A famous episode from the Battle of Put-in-Bay. Perry's flagship, the USS *Lawrence*, had led the American line into battle and had come under heavy fire from Barclay's ships. Battered into hulk, the *Lawrence* had become useless to Perry as a command vessel. Still under heavy fire from the British, Perry decided to shift his flag. He climbed into an exposed boat and had himself rowed over open water to the USS *Niagara*. From the deck of *Niagara*, Perry led the U.S. naval forces to a crushing victory over Barclay and the total loss of the British squadron. ("Perry Leaving the *Lawrence*," from John Richardson, *The War of 1812*, Toronto, 1902 / Library and Archives Canada / C-023695)

By 2:30, both flagships had been pounded to splinters. *Lawrence* was a scene of unimaginable carnage. Eighty-three of 142 officers and men were casualties, and she had only one gun still serviceable. *Detroit* was a similar mess. Barclay had been hit twice, and his second-in-command had been killed. Behind him, the captain of the *Queen Charlotte* was dead and the *Lady Prevost* was veering out of line, her rudder shot away.

The *Niagara* and the American gunboats also pulled into the action. *Niagara* passed in front of the *Detroit*, raking her and the *Queen Charlotte*. With the officers on both dead or wounded, the British ships collided and nothing could be done to organize their disentanglement. The gunboats now brought their terrible heavy guns to bear, and it was not long before Perry's battle fleet was victorious.[127]

The British fleet on Lake Erie was now destroyed. The British possessed not a single combat vessel west of Lake Ontario, leaving every inch of water between Buffalo and Michilimackinac open to the Americans. The fleet built at Erie had fulfilled its first objective, and now it was free to cut off Procter, isolate the north, and wrest control of the upper Great Lakes and hinterland from the British.

When Procter heard the dismal news of Barclay's defeat, he knew the future of his army was bleak. With the lake permanently in American hands, Procter only had an exposed, muddy track to connect him with Lake Ontario and the infrastructure he so badly needed. Already short on regular soldiers, rations for his Native allies and supplies of all kinds for himself, he was forced to retreat.

The British abandoned Detroit, Fort Malden and Amherstburg and began the long retreat up the Thames River. Running through the heart of western Upper Canada, the Thames was the fastest and most secure route to the westernmost end of the Dundas road, which could eventually take Procter's withered army to the safety of Burlington. Harrison, now in complete control of the water highways before him, loaded his men on the ships of Perry's fleet and took off in pursuit.

At the mouth of the Thames, Procter burned what bateaux he did not need. He also burned the *Ellen*, the little ship that Mackintosh and the *Nancy*'s crew had confronted in the mouth of the Sandusky River.[128] With the demise of the *Ellen*, the *Nancy* was the only sailing vessel the British possessed, and the only means of effectively keeping their post at

American shipbuilders launched the USS *Niagara* at Erie, Pennsylvania, in the spring of 1813. *Niagara* saw action at the Battle of Put-in-Bay on 10 September 1813, and served as Sinclair's flagship during his expedition to Lake Huron in the summer of 1814. This reconstruction of the original *Niagara* sails from the port of Erie, Pennsylvania. Here she is seen visiting the Discovery Harbour, a museum dedicated to the nineteenth-century British naval and military establishment at Penetanguishene, Ontario. (Photograph by Harold Russell.)

Michilimackinac open. The future of the North West Company and the Native resistance hinged on the *Nancy* and her cargo.

On board the *Nancy*, Mackintosh knew nothing of these developments. For most of September, Mackintosh and the *Nancy* had been busy ferrying troops and materiel between the northern British and North West Company posts of Michilimackinac, St. Joseph's Island and Sault Ste. Marie. As Procter gathered what remained of his army, and as Tecumseh mustered what few Native supporters were left, the *Nancy* bobbed in ignorant bliss in the cold waters of Lake Huron. No news of the British defeat and retreat reached the isolated northern posts. In early October the *Nancy* set sail once again for Amherstburg, straight into the teeth of the advancing American army of the Northwest.

The *Nancy* took some guests on board for the voyage. A Mr. Reaume was making the trip back to Moy, as was a Mr. David Mitchell, who had come to Mackinac on the *Nancy* at the beginning of August. There was also a British officer, Captain Maxwell, and his family, who were likewise going to rejoin the British garrison.

The *Nancy*, fully laden with passengers and their effects, made the quick run down Lake Huron and reached the entrance to the St. Clair River at two o'clock on Tuesday 4 October. The St. Clair River ran from north to south, with narrow banks and a very strong current. It had taken the *Nancy* days to inch her way up against the river's flow on the way to Michilimackinac, and if the wind was unfavourable the *Nancy* could well end up stuck out of reach of the comforting open waters of the lake. Mackintosh remembered Black Bird's warning that the American fleet had entered Lake Erie. Thus, rather than heading directly into the river, he anchored his vessel about a mile from the mouth of the St. Clair.

Mackintosh did not want to be inching his way back against the current if American forces occupied the banks. Instead of running into the river immediately, at three o'clock he "hoisted the boat out & sent 4 hands with a Mr. Reaume and Tromp on shore to enquire of the Inhabitants what state the country was in about Detroit."[129] Reaume and Tromp then set off to see what kind of news they could bring back to the *Nancy*. The wind was now blowing harder from the north, and Lake Huron was swelling hard. After the boat dropped the two men ashore, it took a heavy wave and filled with water. The boat lost its rudder in this tricky business. But its crew laboured hard in wind and surf and eventually, though only barely, made it back to the *Nancy*.

Two hours later, with the lake still beating heavy waves against the coast, Reaume and Tromp returned with news. Mackintosh tried to send the boat back to pick them up, but with the swells it was impossible for the boat to safely touch shore. Jacob Hammond, the *Nancy*'s first mate, called out across the water for what the two men had learned. Amid the crashing waves and across the yawning distance, Hammond had a hard time making out the reply. He caught enough to know that the Americans had taken a fort, but without the details the men on the *Nancy* could not know which of the many lake forts had fallen.

When Hammond eventually returned on board, Mackintosh called a meeting in his cabin. The *Nancy* was running short on supplies. The same north wind that was frustrating the crew's attempts to pull Reaume and Tromp off the shore was making conditions very favourable for the ship to enter the river. It would also prevent her from exiting the river if she had to. With the waves climbing, and without any guarantee that the Americans were in possession of the banks, Mackintosh, Mitchell, Hammond and Captain Maxwell all agreed to sail under the protection of the banks of the St. Clair.[130]

As the *Nancy*'s crew strained to pull it from the bottom of Lake Huron, the anchor cable snapped. It was a bad omen. Leaving the anchor in the lake, the *Nancy* raced down the river with the wind at its back. By six o'clock that evening, Mackintosh was satisfied that they had gone far enough. He ordered the sails brought in, and when Reaume and Tromp had walked through the forest, he sent the boat over the calm waters of the river to pick them up.[131]

Once on board, Reaume and Tromp could more clearly bring the bad news to Mackintosh and the *Nancy*. It was a catalogue of disasters. The British had been beaten on the lake; the whole fleet had been surrendered to the enemy. Procter had retreated up the Thames, and American forces were now in possession of both Detroit and Amherstburg. With the British retreating far to the east, both banks of the St. Clair River would be firmly in American hands. The *Nancy* could not return to Moy, and would have to try and escape from the river as soon as possible despite being short on provisions. That evening, Mackintosh set off to the British Canadian side of the river to see what further information he could get himself. More disturbing details reached his ears. "All the public Buildings were burnt at both Detroit and Amherstburg," he later reported, and "all the Indians had joined or made peace with the Americans."[132] To make matters worse, downstream two schooners and two gunboats of the United States Navy were lying in wait for the *Nancy*. The British defeat seemed total, and because of limited visibility, the St. Clair River was no place for the *Nancy*. Mackintosh returned on board at eleven o'clock in the evening, when it was too late to make a run back to Lake Huron. Instead, Mackintosh posted a man on both sides of the ship to keep a close watch on the riverbanks — the pathways of the enemy — during the night.[133]

While the situation seemed dismal to Mackintosh and his crew, they did not know that even worse news was brewing further east. Procter's withered army was struggling up the Thames, accompanied by a few hundred Native warriors under Tecumseh, and with Harrison's Kentucky mounted infantry hard on its heels. That night they encamped near a Moravian mission village near what is now London, Ontario. The following morning, Harrison's army caught what was left of the British and Native army. In a quick battle, the Kentucky mounted infantry broke the exhausted lines of the British regulars, then turned its full force against Tecumseh and his warriors.

Tecumseh, the great organizer of Native resistance, was killed — and with him the hope for an independent Indian state somewhere in the heartland of America. Many of his comrades also died. Twenty-eight British officers were killed or captured, along with over six hundred men. Of Procter's entire army, only about two hundred and fifty struggled back to Burlington.[134] The Americans now controlled every inch of territory for more than one hundred and fifty miles around the spot where the *Nancy* had gently dropped her anchor.

The next day, 5 October, a Wednesday, brought the *Nancy* a friendly visitor. "At daylight of this day an Indian comes on board who had the evening before fallen in with Reaume." Mackintosh was eager to confirm more about the American occupation and the extent of their hold on the local area. He took the Native up on an offer to help the isolated British vessel. "At my request [the man] went down on the British side of the river to see if any gunboats where coming up."[135]

At the battle of Moraviantown, Upper Canada, 5 October 1813, American forces under Brigadier General William Henry Harrison defeated the British under Major General Henry Procter and allied Natives under Tecumseh. The American victory marked the end of the British occupation of Michigan and denied the British use of the Detroit River supply route. The death of Tecumseh dealt a major blow to the Native confederacy and brought several Native nations into alliance with the Americans. ("Battle of Thames," artist William Emmons / Library and Archives Canada / C-041031)

With the danger of the *Nancy* being ambushed in the narrow river, the passengers wanted to get off the vessel as soon as possible. They went ashore to find some extra boats to help move their possessions to the riverbank. While they were still ashore, the Native returned from his scouting mission, "saying that there were some Americans on horse on the way up." A half hour ticked by as Mackintosh nervously waited for the cavalry to appear. Then Mackintosh ordered Tromp to go ashore, "to proceed down as far as Sambrinards & not to return unless he saw the enemy advancing."[136] With his own sentry posted, the *Nancy* continued to help its civilian passengers pack up.

Tromp had not been gone long when a group of men appeared on the American (west) riverbank below the *Nancy*. Mackintosh, convinced that the American horsemen had appeared, began to prepare to blow up the *Nancy*. With the Americans already in control of Lake Erie, the capture of the *Nancy* would add to American naval strength and only increase the ability of Harrison's army to attack Michilimackinac. With Procter retreating up the Thames River, the fur-trading post was the last British outpost in the Northwest, and the last obstacle to American domination of the upper Great Lakes, the fur trade, and the Northwest Native nations.

The passengers hurried ashore to the west bank, where the Americans easily captured them. Mackintosh wrote, "I soon after saw a canoe crossing below with a white flag & as full as they could cram."[137] At one o'clock in the afternoon, not long after their passengers were in American hands and safely out of harm's way, the Americans called for the *Nancy* to surrender.

"Some person sung out from the woods to surrender the vessel, that my property & that of the men's should not be touched," Mackintosh wrote. "I hailed in turn to know whom it was, when the person stepped & again repeated the same thing."[138] The wind had changed direction that night, and instead of blowing from the north, as it had when the *Nancy* had entered the river, it had veered south and died to a light breeze. Mackintosh, a canny mariner with a keen weather eye, noted that the wind was slowly increasing and that the *Nancy* was making some headway against the strong river current. There was now the possibility of the *Nancy* escaping up river, if the Americans could be

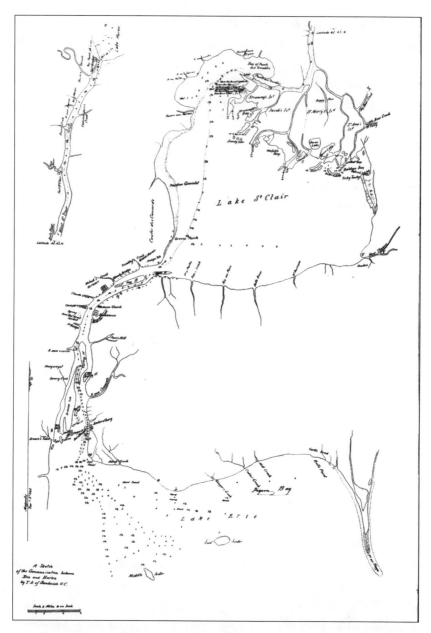

Lake Huron's waters flow south, through St. Clair River to Lake St. Clair, then Detroit River to Lake Erie. Based at Moy, opposite Detroit, the *Nancy* made extensive use of these waterways in her role as private and government transport. American militia ambushed the *Nancy* in the St. Clair River (shown in the inset) in the fall of 1813. ("A sketch of the communications between Erie and Huron," by Thomas Smith / Library and Archives Canada / NMC 3241)

held off long enough for the little schooner to make it to the freedom of the lake.

Mackintosh went ashore to talk to the Americans. Their tough, tactful commander was a lieutenant colonel of the militia by the name of Beaubien. Backed up by his men, Beaubien once again insisted that the *Nancy* surrender and pledged that he would gladly guarantee the property of its crew — they would lose nothing and save their lives. Mackintosh needed to buy time. He asked for an hour to consider the ultimatum, and returned to the ship. It was a good offer, but Mackintosh had other ideas. With the *Nancy* headed north, he was able to move both of the six-pounders to the port side of the vessel, where they could be brought to bear against the Americans lurking on the wooded bank. Mackintosh, with a leader's zeal, then spelled out the situation for his men. They could surrender the *Nancy*, and give her and her cargo to the Americans. Or they could fight. To a man, the *Nancy*'s crew pledged to fight for the ship. With the guns ready, Mackintosh went back to Beaubien.[139]

Beaubien was not pleased with Mackintosh's dismissal of his offer. He claimed to have fifty men under his command and threatened to open fire on the exposed little schooner the moment Mackintosh moved to sail up river. A defiant Mackintosh told him he would shoot back, spun around on his heels and returned to his vessel.

The moment the *Nancy*'s men began hauling in the anchor, the American shore erupted with small arms fire. Shots flicked at the sails and chipped the booms and masts. True to their word, the inexperienced fighters on the *Nancy* returned fire. Swabbing, loading and firing the guns, the *Nancy*'s men thumped away against the wooded shoreline. One sailor, Joseph Paquet, was burned when some of the guns' cartridges accidentally exploded on deck. For a moment, the mainsail caught fire, but the quick-thinking crew soon doused the flames.

After fifteen minutes of exchanging fire, the Americans had had enough. "They then escaped & went off, whether for want of powder or that we had killed or wounded any of them I know not."[140] Mackintosh and his men had no time to contemplate the battle. They quickly fished in the anchor, then, with the wind out of the southwest, they crawled upstream to the rapids, the last obstacle before reaching open water.

As the sun began to set, the *Nancy*'s crew lashed a stout tracking line to the shoreline. Hauling hard on it, they tried to pull the schooner over the St. Clair rapids. It was exhausting work against a swift current, and after two hours of trying to force the *Nancy* upstream, Mackintosh decided to shift tactics. He dropped anchor and decided to wait for a stronger breeze to help them up into the lake.

At ten o'clock that night, with the *Nancy* in such a vulnerable position, the Americans again made entreaties to Mackintosh. This time Beaubien sent the captured civilian Reaume aboard the *Nancy*, bearing a letter that reiterated the kind offer of protection to private property. The Americans, with fine talk and sensible promises, had made a deep and lasting impression on the fur traders and the captive Captain Maxwell. Reaume advised Mackintosh that both he and Maxwell thought that Mackintosh would be better off tossing the prized gunpowder overboard and surrendering the schooner. Let her pass into Yankee hands, ran the strains of the half-hearted. It was enough to convince the first mate, Hammond. He told Mackintosh that there was no way they could escape. He said that they should give up the *Nancy*.

Held in the grip of the strong St. Clair rapids, Mackintosh had few options. His first mate and two of his now-captured passengers were advising him that the opposing force was too strong to resist. But the dogged Mackintosh would have none of it. He clung to a sense of obligation to king and country that is undeniable and had a burning zeal that kept him warm in the worst of circumstances. He weighed the odds, then decided to fight. "I replied that I would never heave any public property overboard to save private," Mackintosh noted. "Let the consequences be what they will, I will attempt to get into the lake & go for Makinac."[141]

After a final warning, Reaume returned to shore, his mission a failure. Mackintosh now doubled the *Nancy*'s watch and went down to his cabin for the night. He could not sleep. If Beaubien and his men were close enough to send Reaume with a letter demanding capitulation, then his force must surely be close enough to mount an attack by land or by water. Mackintosh's every sense was strained as he waited for the call to come on deck, for the call to respond to Beaubien's threat, for the call to defend the *Nancy*. All night he tossed and turned. He listened as Jonas Parker tried to call Hammond on deck for his turn at watch, and listened as the unnerved, discontented Hammond refused. It rained a little, but the wind was still too soft to take them up the river.

By daybreak, however, no Americans had shown themselves. Mackintosh, eyeing the weather gauge, watching the barometer fall, called all hands to deck and had the canvas stretched to take in the strengthening morning breeze. After forty-five minutes of fighting the rapids, the *Nancy*'s bow cut through the last of the current, and at eight o'clock in the morning on Thursday, 7 October, she made her return to Lake Huron.

The crew cheered. After forty-eight gruelling hours of hard labour, combat and suspense on the St. Clair River, they were finally free of the rising American threat and able to run to the protection of Michilimackinac. They fired three guns in celebration and headed back to where they had left their best anchor sitting on the bottom of the lake. They found it again, fished it, and brought it back on board. Buoyed by success, Mackintosh headed the *Nancy* north by west, and had all sail set.

Her fortune did not last. Fair wind turned to foul: by eleven o'clock that morning, the wind swung to the west-northwest. It built to a gale, and showers began to pelt the beleaguered little vessel. The next day, the wind shifted again, blowing straight this time from the northwest — from the direction of Michilimackinac. Mackintosh tacked the *Nancy*, bringing her back and forth across the wind to edge her closer to her destination. With full sail kit clapped on, *Nancy* made good speed through the water. Hail shot down into her wooden decks, and when Mackintosh tacked back to the westward the gunwales were awash in water.

For the next five days the storm grew in intensity and held the schooner in its grip. Mackintosh and his little crew battled to keep the *Nancy* afloat. Winds from the northwest ripped at the stays and the sails. Snow, rain and sleet whipped the crew as it struggled to splice together the disintegrating rigging and repair canvas. By Monday, 11 October, the pump was kept going every two hours. Later that day, land was spotted twelve miles distant.

The gale was blowing so strongly that it was driving the *Nancy* toward the dangerous rocky coast near the Saginaw River. Early next morning, Hammond again spotted land to their lee. Mackintosh ordered the leads out, and found the *Nancy* in only fourteen fathoms of water. He ordered spare anchors readied, hoping that they would stop the schooner from being smashed against the cutting shoreline. By the time the anchors were in the bows, only seven and a half fathoms stood between her and lake bottom.

Mackintosh ordered the anchors dropped. The cables snaked quickly out as the *Nancy* pitched closer and closer to the shoreline. The schooner came wildly about when the anchors finally dug into the bottom and surged bow-on into the blowing gale. The crew then rushed to secure the ship against the deadly winds. The sails were hauled in and the anchor cables wound tightly around the mainmast so as to keep them secure and free from flapping in the wild wind.

Mackintosh, the ultimate sailor of windswept seas, puts it this way: "Got the square sail booms in upon deck, bent a new hawser to the Kedge & let it go under foot, battened down the Hatches, braced the yards fore and aft, cleared the Boat & got the oars ready — in short made every thing as snug as possible — for on the squalls clearing away we could distinctly see the breakers astern about a cable length distant, the land appearing about 2 miles."[142]

Now there was nothing Mackintosh and the ship's company could do but wait for the October storm to blow itself out. The ship had been short on provisions before she entered the St. Clair River; now, days later, the sailors found themselves down to their last morsels of pork, mutton and biscuit. At daylight on Tuesday, Mackintosh could clearly see the danger: nothing but shoals lay between the *Nancy* and the shoreline. More squalls struck the *Nancy* and frustrated Mackintosh's attempts to pull the schooner closer to its anchors. Sleet and rain came on in unremitting fashion, and hail pummelled the ship. Mackintosh gave up for the day and retired to his cabin to wait out the blasts and foul weather.

On Wednesday, the storm seemed to let up a little. "For the first time the weather cleared up to enable us to see some distance," Mackintosh wrote dejectedly, "when we could perceive nothing but shoals & Islands as far as the eye could carry."[143] More squalls came that night, and the *Nancy*, tugging at her anchors, continued to heave in the heavy, white-capped waves. The ship, which had fought for life in the narrow St. Clair River, was now fighting for life in the worst that Lake Huron had to throw at her.

The next day, fully a week after escaping the river, the storm abated around noon. Mackintosh put his men to work repairing the ship, getting it ready to move out from the piercing coastline. That afternoon, a canoe with three Natives pulled out from the shore and, after the *Nancy* hoisted flag, came alongside. Mackintosh learned he was only eighty miles from the mouth of the St. Clair, near La Cloche, where the North West Company had a trading post. By that evening the wind had swung to the southwest, blowing gently, and the *Nancy* hauled in her anchors, made sail and gingerly headed west.

Friday morning the *Nancy* sighted the Michigan coastline and headed for the gap between St. Joseph's and Michilimackinac. On Saturday the *Nancy* was in the fur-trade highway, and found canoes laden with fur-trade goods going both west, to Mackinac, and east to the French River and the St. Lawrence. Mackintosh hailed two canoes and got one of them to carry letters to Montreal and the other dispatches to Captain Bullock at Michilimackinac. Sunday found the *Nancy* still steering west, finally closing in on the safe haven.

The weather was not done with the *Nancy* yet. As the schooner neared Bois Blanc Island, a fresh gale blew from the west. Once again, the anchors came out and the *Nancy* rode the pounding waves, this time in only two fathoms of water. The mainsail was shredded in the wind. When the weather cleared that morning, the *Nancy* was only four miles from Mackinac.

The wind kept to the west. On Monday, Mackintosh tried to tack the *Nancy* through the wind but was forced to drop his anchors again. Only a short distance from the safety of Michilmackinac, Mackintosh was forced to wait. While riding at anchor, he wrote to Captain Bullock, explaining Procter's defeat and his own near-capture in the St. Clair River.[144] On Tuesday, 19 October, there was more snow, and Mackintosh had all the nonessential goods and gunpowder thrown overboard. But it was the last day of the ordeal. The gale-battered *Nancy* eventually limped into the harbour at Michilimackinac, rigging and sails mauled by nine days at the mercy of Lake Huron.[145]

Meanwhile, at Detroit, Harrison was consolidating his position after his victory on the Thames River. Never a man to lose time, Harrison had entered into peace negotiations with the Native nations of the Michigan area. With Procter in retreat and Lake Erie in American hands, the Natives were cut off from their war supplies. Several Native groups that had formerly been allied with the British exited the war, including several Potawatomi, Wyandot, Miami, Ottawa and Chippewa groups.[146] Harrison then began to make preparations for the final stages of Chauncey's plan, and ordered a force readied for the recapture of Michilimackinac. As Chauncey had surmised, the seizure of the island would, in one month, have completely tipped the scales of the war in the Northwest in America's favour. Harrison would not only have regained all of the United States' pre-war territory, but also some of western Upper Canada. More importantly, he could cut the remaining Natives of the Northwest off from their British suppliers and force them into peace.

These plans were foiled, however, when the very same storm that had nearly wrecked the *Nancy* swept through the area. "I am sorry to inform you that from the effects of a violent storm there is now no prospect of accomplishing that desirable object, the reduction of Michilimackinac, this season," Harrison wrote to the Secretary of War. "Upon consultation with the two Brigadiers and Commodore Perry and Captain Elliot, it was unanimously determined that the season is too far advanced to attempt an expedition to Mackinack if it were not commenced in two or three days, and there was not hopes of supplies being obtained in that time."[147] The same storm that had nearly been the end of the *Nancy* also saved Michilimackinac for the British, for the time being.

All was not rosy at Michilimackinac. Thirteen canoes loaded with provisions had landed there on 9 October, but they were destined to be supplies and presents for the Natives of the Northwest. No matter how desperate the garrison was for supplies, William McKay and Robert Dickson, the senior Indian agents, were under strict instructions to keep the goods flowing to their Native allies, and they obeyed their instructions and forwarded all the goods to the posts on Lake Michigan for distribution. When Procter's loss and the full extent of Michilimackinac's precariousness became known, McKay suggested that Bullock try and buy supplies from the few settlers in the Green Bay area. Bullock agreed, and McKay organized an expedition. Dickson also told Bullock that supplies had been forwarded to the secret British depot on Matchedash Bay, in the southeastern corner of Midland Bay, a minor annex of Georgian Bay.[148]

Hearing this, Bullock ordered Mackintosh and the *Nancy* back out onto the lake to secure the supplies at Matchedash Bay. Linked to York by the same route that carried goods down the Nottawasaga River, Matchedash had the advantage of being little known, well-protected by a rocky entrance, and hard to find. The Commissary General had been tinkering with both the Nottawasaga route and the new Matchedash Bay depot as alternate supply routes to Michilimackinac. Now that the *Nancy* had returned empty-handed from Amherstburg, Bullock desperately needed the supplies to be brought as quickly as possible from Georgian Bay.

As much as he wished to answer in the affirmative to this urgent call to duty, Mackintosh had to refuse the order. The *Nancy*'s sails and rigging could not withstand any more strain on the open lake, and he simply could not risk endangering her in the late-autumn storms that were predictably savage and often fatal. On 28 October, an examining committee agreed wholeheartedly with Mackintosh. "The only good sails she has," the committee concluded, "are the two topgallant sails, square sail & one cable. — The fore top-, main Top-, fore-, & main-sails, jibs, and one cable, unserviceable."[149] Given this ruling, Mackintosh then sailed the *Nancy* to the yard at Sault Ste. Marie for the winter, where the North West Company could give her a complete refitting. That winter, Mackintosh and his men would work hard to rehabilitate the battered *Nancy*.

With the *Nancy* out of commission for the autumn, Bullock tried one last desperate gamble to get enough food for the winter. He ordered two canoes and one bateau, manned by Natives and militia, to head for Matchedash Bay and bring back supplies. The oldest and most experienced fur traders knew that the weather on Lake Huron could be unpredictable and severe at that time of year. It was a long journey, and winter would soon descend upon the upper Great Lakes. Nevertheless, Bullock was determined, given the dire food situation, to risk the expedition to Georgian Bay. Two large fur-trader canoes and bateaux were fitted out and manned by Natives and members of the local militia. Command was given to a sergeant of the 10th Royal Veterans and an interpreter with the Indian

Department. On 28 October the expedition set out over the frigid autumn waters of Lake Huron.

The weather soon turned on them, as it had turned on Mackintosh and the *Nancy*. After five days of frost, snowstorms and hacking their way through newly forming ice, the bateaux and one canoe, commanded by the sergeant of the 10th Royal Veterans, turned around and returned to Michilimackinac.

The other canoe persevered. When the weather reached its worst, the interpreter and the Natives in that canoe headed for some Native settlements on the north shore of Lake Huron. There they waited out some of the worst of the weather, and when the lake seemed calm enough to proceed they set off for Matchedash Bay. On 15 November, over two weeks after their departure, they finally made it to the secluded British base. There, they found that no supplies had been forwarded for the garrison at Michilimackinac. They had forced their way through the oncoming Canadian winter for nothing. Bitterly disappointed that their exhausting journey had been for naught, the Natives and the interpreter were soon faced with another problem. Ice had begun to form over the lake, and if they did not return to Michilimackinac soon, they risked being iced in at Matchedash Bay. With no other choice, the hardy men launched their canoe once more. They finally arrived back at Michilimackinac, cold, hungry and frostbitten, on 2 December.[150] Bullock's last-ditch attempt had failed, and the inhabitants of Michilimackinac tightened their belts for the coming winter. Meanwhile, the Americans made urgent efforts to repair and ready their great fleet. At Erie, the captured, battered Royal Navy vessels and the new American ships were slung in over the sandbar. Once again, Secretary of War John Armstrong's plan to attack such vital British locales as Montreal or Kingston was rejected in favour of a more methodical plan of attack from the west. The Niagara Peninsula was to be made the priority, so that an American army under General Jacob Brown could capture Burlington and York. In the meantime, Michilimackinac could be isolated and the Northwest captured for the United States.[151]

It was a somewhat unwieldy plan. As one American officer, grumbling about the army's handling of the war, put it, "Montreal is the Root at which the Axe should have been first directed — cut off the communication from their resources, and the upper province must fall of course, instead of which they begun at the wrong end, for were they to beat them at the upper end of the province and continue to drive them down, unless there was a force in their rear, they would be like a Snow ball, daily accumulating as they rolled back."[152] Michilimackinac, at the upper reaches of the province, was tying up the American efforts to roll up Upper Canada. If the British could hold on to the Gibraltar of the north, enemy resourcers would continue to be siphoned away from critical focal points — but only, that is, if they had enough supplies to outlast the Americans. As the ice broke that spring, the little British force would come under attack from two directions, and the *Nancy* would become the centre of attention.

A Fiery End for the *Nancy*

For the British in the Northwest, the winter of 1813–14 was gloomy at best. Supplies had run out, and as the only large vessel on Lake Huron, the *Nancy* had taken on a new importance since the previous fall. As Mackintosh had discovered, the St. Clair River route was now closed to British shipping. Two alternatives remained. The first was up the North West Company road to Lake Simcoe, where supplies could be carried to Lake Huron via the Nottawasaga River. The second was the French River route, which was only accessible by canoe for most of the journey. Thus the former, the York–Lake Simcoe–Nottawasaga River line, was adopted as the primary means of resupplying Michilimackinac in 1814. That January, Deputy Assistant Commissary General George Crookshank reported to Major General Gordon Drummond that a short road could be cut between the lake and the Nottawasaga River. From there, a supply depot could be built where provisions could be loaded onto a boat at the mouth of the river. The British also eyed a place on Penetanguishene Bay, a spot thirty miles from Lake Simcoe, which would take considerably more time to connect by road to the British supply lines.[153]

By 1814 the strain on the British supply system had become critical. Local farms could not feed the thousands of sailors and soldiers that the war had brought to the upper province. Furthermore, repeated militia call-ups had disrupted the normal agricultural cycle, and in a region like

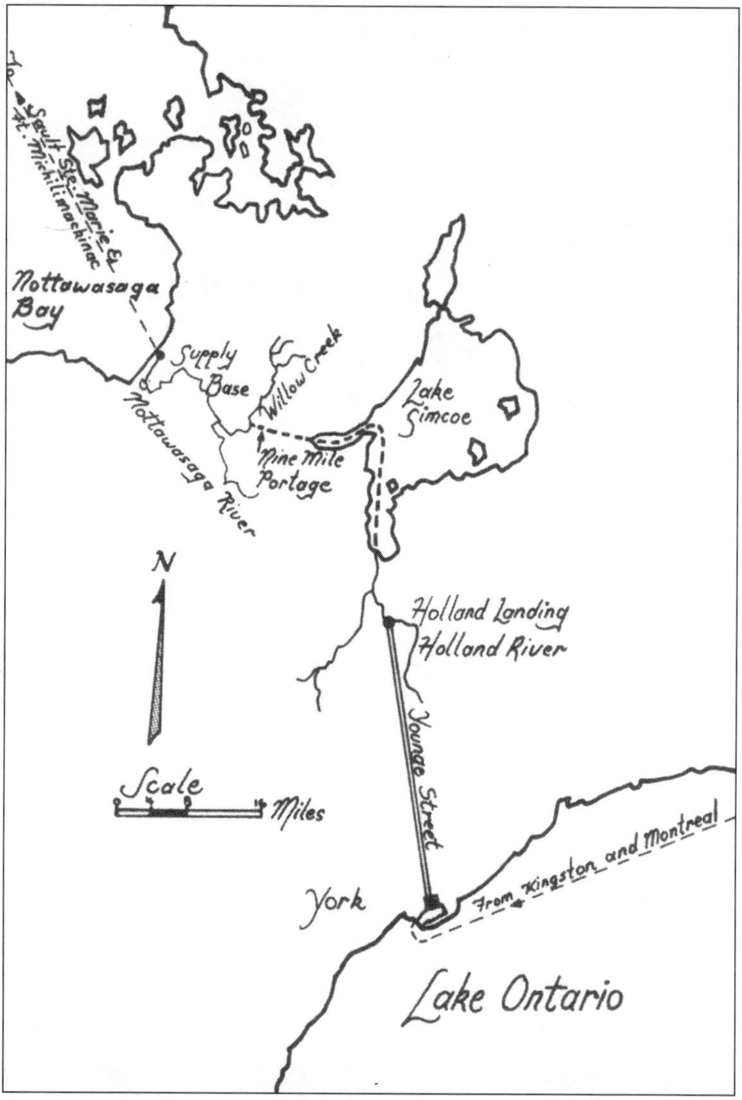
To Sault Ste. Marie &
Ft. Michilimackinac
Nottawasaga
Bay
Supply
Base
Willow Creek
Lake
Simcoe
Nine Mile
Portage
Nottawasaga River
N
Holland Landing
Holland River
Younge Street
Scale
Miles
York
From Kingston and Montreal
Lake Ontario

The defeat at Moraviantown on 5 October 1813 closed the Detroit River to the British. Consequently, the supply route running from York (now Toronto) to Lake Simcoe and from Lake Simcoe via the Nottawasaga became the primary supply line for the British forces on Lake Huron. The *Nancy* kept up her freighting duties between the mouth of the Nottawasaga and Michilimackinac in 1814, ferrying supplies, messages and officers and men to the isolated garrison. (From *HMS Nancy and the War of 1812*, 1978)

Upper Canada this only meant that there was additional pressure on the British government to supply its troops from outside the province. The smuggling of food from Vermont and other sympathetic states increased, as did the amount of food imported through Quebec and distributed over the British Army's supply network.

Deeply laden bateaux from Quebec had to make the dangerous run up the St. Lawrence River, skirting the American border, to Kingston. From the Royal Navy post there, the goods and supplies could be taken either by bateaux or by sailing vessel along Lake Ontario to York, and from there to Niagara or north to the Nottawasaga River route. The Lake Ontario route was, of course, especially dangerous when Chauncey and the American fleet were out and looking for British vessels to intercept. The result was that Drummond's whole supply line was tenuous, and he constantly worried about how to provision his troops.[154]

The *Nancy* was vital as the last link in this vast supply network that connected Michilimackinac to Quebec. As the only serviceable sailing vessel on Lake Huron, the *Nancy* was the most efficient and the safest way of bringing badly needed goods to the Northwest. With her deep hold, the schooner could ferry food and provisions to the Michilimackinac garrison, which would keep the Natives of the Northwest in the war and fighting for the British side. Without her, there would be no way to maintain the garrison.

It had been a hard winter at Michilimackinac. With the capture of Amherstburg the previous fall, no new government supplies had been dispatched there. Captain Bullock, who had just made the trip to Mackinac in the *Nancy* himself, realized the outpost had only a month's worth of food on hand when the news of Procter's defeat reached him.[155]

Bullock had set about immediately buying what food he could from the neighbouring settlements. There was enough corn and fish, but he calculated that his meat supply, even on reduced rations, would only last until March. He had no extra clothing for his men, and the last of the available pay was issued to the men on 28 January.[156] When the *Nancy* had arrived the previous October, there had been few supplies available to them, aside from 200 pounds of salt pork — no fresh vegetables, rum, or anything else.[157] With the prospect of four months of nothing to eat but salted pork, the winter indeed seemed gloomy.

Prevost, realizing the strategic value of Mackinac, dispatched a new commanding officer there. Bullock, who to that point had acted admirably under the circumstances, was to give way to a vastly more experienced officer. Lieutenant Colonel Robert McDouall[158] of the Glengarry Light Infantry set out in February to take command of Michilimackinac and the British forces of the Northwest. A career military officer like Procter and Brock, McDouall had served in the British army since his teens. Prior to his posting to Canada, he had seen action in the Caribbean. For the first year of the war, McDouall was an official aide to Prevost, during which time he developed strong administrative capabilities. His skills were rewarded in 1813 when he was chosen to present captured American flags to the British court in London.[159] Upon his return to Canada, Prevost gave him the challenge of commanding the most isolated and valuable post in wilderness British North America.

McDouall did not arrive at Michilimackinac empty-handed. He brought with him £1,500 to pay the back salaries of the soldiers at the little fort, with the promise of more money to buy food and clothing.[160] He also brought with him Lieutenant Newdigate Poyntz, of the Royal Navy, and twenty Royal Navy seamen to take over everything that floated on Lake Huron. The Royal Navy had officially taken responsibility for the Provincial Marine on 22 April 1813. For the rest of that year, James Yeo and Robert Barclay, professional Royal Navy officers, had supervised the naval activities on lakes Champlain, Ontario and Erie. Until Barclay's defeat, however, they had left the transport ships on the upper Great Lakes as private vessels. But maintaining Michilimackinac had become too vital a task to be left in private hands. The officers and sailors McDouall brought with him were there to give the vessels on Lake Huron the Royal Navy's professional edge.

McDouall also brought with him a keen understanding of the logistical situation. McDouall and his party had taken the Nottawasaga route to Michilimackinac that spring. While the snow still crusted the ground, McDouall had marched his party from York to Lake Simcoe, and from thence over the portage to the Nottawasaga. It was when his men were encamped at the upper reaches of the river that McDouall spied an opportunity. He ordered the construction of a small supply depot. Eight log warehouses, a sawpit and a blockhouse were all enclosed by a sturdy wooden palisade. Named Fort Willow, after the adjacent creek, the small stockade was a key military strategy.

Hidden at the very upper reaches of the Nottawasaga, Fort Willow allowed goods, supplies and ammunition to be stockpiled before their long journey over Lake Huron to Michilimackinac. It not only served as a supply depot, but also as a building depot. Bateaux — large, shallow, sturdy rowboats capable of carrying much cargo — could be constructed at Fort Willow and used to carry goods down the Nottawasaga. If need be, the bateaux could also be taken over the rough waters of the inland seas to carry the goods straight to Michilimackinac. Fort Willow gave McDouall security on his supply line, an all-important consideration if he was to command the most distant and isolated British fort along the entire American frontier.

All was not lost, however. On the horizon, there were glimmers of hope for the British, and dark clouds for the Americans. In March, the allied armies captured Paris. On 4 April Napoleon abdicated, and Britain was suddenly free of her largest and most dangerous enemy. Thousands of British redcoats and hundreds of Royal Navy vessels could now be turned to the defence of Britain's North American colonies.

The news shocked Washington. Reports of British preparations to send the Duke of Wellington's victorious army to North America meant that the United States was running out of time to affect its conquest of Canada. Preparations were hurried along. A final stab at Upper Canada, across the Niagara Peninsula, was planned. To divide the Natives of the northwest from their British allies, Michilimackinac would have to be retaken.

Mackintosh and the crew of the *Nancy*, meanwhile, spent a cabin-feverish winter huddled next to the St. Mary's rapids, near Sault Ste. Marie. They built a little cabin near the frozen river and nicknamed it "the house." They received a shipment of salt, which they used to preserve the meat of several cows and pigs they slaughtered over the course of the winter, and periodically broached a keg of rum. [161]

Besides simply surviving a northern winter, the ship's company — number eight in all — was busy repairing its stout schooner in preparation for the next season's campaigning. Jonas Parker, the carpenter, and

Joseph Lamotte, his mate, organized the rest of crew into work details. They began by stripping her of all her sails, rigging and topmasts. Items beyond repair were set aside and new ones were fashioned. The men dug a sawpit and cut new planks for their schooner, carved new topmasts and booms, and replaced what decking and fittings they could. They also cut firewood for themselves and for the nearby North West Company post.[162]

The *Nancy*'s crew also took on a pet winter project. The North West Company schooner *Mink* had run aground in the river and been abandoned. With the vital shortage of supply vessels, everything that could float counted. Mackintosh and his men put their seagoing experience to work on the *Mink*. Carpenter Parker made some skids, and when the water level was right the men tried to shove them under the vessel so that they could more easily push her into open water. Unfortunately, the harsh winter soon defeated their efforts. Ice soon gripped their skids, and after moving the *Mink* only ten feet, Mackintosh and the men of the *Nancy* had to give up on her.[163] The effort was not all in vain, however. That spring the *Mink* was floated, and the *Nancy* had a sister ship on the upper lakes.

The confined quarters and endless work strained the already-frayed nerves of the *Nancy*'s crew. Tempers had already been short when the *Nancy* reached Sault Ste. Marie: the stress of war had already put the crabby and pessimistic Hammond on edge, and soon after the *Nancy* was put up for the winter, discontent spread throughout the crew. "This morning had some words with Jacob Hammond, Richard McGregor & John Morrison for not being at work at an early hour," Mackintosh wrote angrily. "They are very insolent. Morrison & I have a scuffle."[164] The early fisticuffs between Mackintosh and one of his crew did not bode well for a long winter. McGregor threatened not to cut more than a cord of wood, and Hammond went a step further, claiming he would not cut more than he needed for himself.

By the spring, things had not improved. The provisions had dwindled, and the lack of dietary variety only played on the men's cabin fever. McGregor wanted the crew to kill some of the North West Company's cattle and have fresh beef, rather than eat their own salted rations. When Mackintosh asked Evan Richards, the cook, to give the crew breakfast at sunrise, they complained that he was trying to work them too hard.

Hammond tried to convince him not to send them to work outside, complaining "that it is damn hard to be working in the snow."[165] Mackintosh tried to make up for the harsh conditions by keeping his men busy. Hammond counted the days until his contract was up in June.

When the ice broke and the *Nancy* was freed from its wintry prison, Mackintosh steered her back to Michilimakinac. Until this time, the *Nancy* had been acting as a hired transport to the British forces. Despite the dangers she had faced, the *Nancy* had still been — on paper — a civilian vessel. That spring, however, she was officially transferred to the Royal Navy. The North West Company schooner *Nancy* was now His Majesty's Schooner *Nancy*, and Lieutenant Poyntz was in command. While Mackintosh was no longer captain of the vessel, he stayed on as her sailing master.[166]

Unfortunately, McDouall detested Poyntz, and it was more than a matter of army versus navy. While Yeo described Poyntz as "a very intelligent active officer,"[167] McDouall described him as "the pertinacious Lieut that [Yeo] unfortunately sent me." Even as they had crossed the ice together that winter, Poyntz had irritated McDouall, and in a mere matter of months Poyntz had succeeded in fully provoking one of Prevost's picked men into asking for his replacement. McDouall raged to Major General Drummond, commander of the British forces in Upper Canada, that Poyntz was "full of his own consequence, as Commanding on Lake Huron (Commanding what? not a vessel) and a great stickler for naval etiquette, is constantly disposed to cavil and on the watch for opportunities in his naval capacity, to oppose what I wish."[168]

What McDouall wanted to do was to cut the *Nancy* down into a gunboat so that it could deal with an American naval threat to Michilimackinac. With the shortage of supplies and the reality that, even with extra cannon, she could still not challenge any of the Erie-built American ships, both Mackintosh and Poyntz protested at the idea. McDouall, grumbling, relented, but he complained to Prevost nonetheless. The *Nancy* was left as a supply schooner.

The inter-service friction was doing nothing for the security of Michilimackinac. McDouall blamed Poyntz for not getting the *Nancy* ready that spring, and for the delays in getting the vessel out on the lake for supplies. "Indeed I should have sent [Poyntz] back in her, only I

A career U.S. naval officer, Arthur Sinclair served on Lake Ontario during the first two years of the War of 1812. He took command of the American Lake Erie squadron in the spring of 1814, with glory awaiting him. Sinclair led the American expedition to Lake Huron in the summer of 1814 and, to his disappointment, unsuccessfully attacked the British garrison at Michilimackinac. Sinclair's forces torched and completely wasted the Nor'Westers post at Sault Ste Marie. On 14 August 1814 Sinclair discovered the *Nancy* hiding in the Nottawasaga River, and the resulting battle led to the schooner's destruction. ("Commodore Arthur Sinclair," artist unknown / Naval Historical Centre / NH 44925)

could not spare in our circumstances, the twenty Seamen, and they were not willing to serve under a military officer."[169] With Poyntz as its commander, the *Nancy* only got underway for the first time in late May.

The *Nancy* made several trips back and forth to the Nottawasaga River mouth, ferrying supplies, ammunition, and even two companies of the Royal Newfoundland Regiment to Michilmackinac. Despite these efforts, the first few supply runs were extremely disappointing to McDouall. He not only had to supply his own troops, but, given the poverty of the local crops, he was also responsible for feeding his Native allies. With the scarcity of supplies at Michilimackinac, he was being forced to withhold food from the hungry wives and children of the Native warriors just so that he could keep his own garrison and the warriors fed at partial rations. On one occasion, in early July, the *Nancy* arrived from the Nottawasaga with only eleven barrels of provisions for the garrison in her hold. Exasperated, McDouall begged for more supplies, and the commissary general promised him two hundred barrels' worth by 20 July. McDouall instantly sent the *Nancy* back to the Nottawasaga for them.[170]

Meanwhile, in the spring of 1814, the American fleet on Lake Erie received a new commander. Captain Arthur Sinclair had spent the previous two years cruising with Chauncey's squadron on Lake Ontario, and was burning for the opportunity to see action and distinguish himself. That winter, Sinclair had retired from the Lake Ontario squadron and gone home to Wilmington, Virginia, where he lobbied for command of a frigate on the Atlantic coast. For a time, it seemed he might be given command of a gunboat flotilla in Norfolk.[171] Then he was abruptly sent north again, to take command of the Lake Erie fleet. By the end of April 1814 he was at Erie as commodore, reorganizing and outfitting his flotilla.[172]

American war plans for 1814 mirrored those of the autumn of 1813. The Secretary of War outlined a four-stage plan for the capture of Canada. First, the Americans were to sweep the British from the upper Great Lakes by recapturing Michilimackinac and destroying all the other posts. Second, the Lake Erie fleet was to land an army on the north shore of Lake Erie and supply it. Third, the army would seize Burlington, a move that would cut off the British army on the Niagara Peninsula and yield a clear line of advance to York and

Kingston. Fourth, the Lake Ontario squadron would then help the army to solidify its hold on the peninsula or to capture Kingston. In either event, the Americans would be able, according to the plan drawn up by the War Department, to "take a new line of operation from Fort George to Lake Simcoe, shutting out the enemy from all direct communication with the western lakes and thus destroying his means of sustaining his western posts and settlements and of reinstating his influence over Indian wants and policy."[173] The American plan of attack was the worst nightmare of the North West Company, the Native tribes and the British.

The American plan was also an obvious one. When Commodore Sinclair wrote to Lieutenant Colonel George Croghan — formerly a major and Procter's nemesis at Fort Stephenson, and now American commander at Detroit — Croghan had already taken steps to ensure the success of an American operation in the Northwest. "Knowing that an expedition would be fitted out against the posts on the upper lakes," Croghan informed Sinclair, "I was enabled to anticipate your enquiries relative to the situation, strength & c. of those several places, and have taken such steps as are most likely to secure me correct information on the subject."[174] Croghan did not have the all the facts at his fingertips, but he assured Sinclair that the garrisons at St. Joseph's, Sault Ste. Marie, and Mackinac were very weakly defended. He sent out additional spies to gather more information about the British activities on Lake Simcoe, the Nottawasaga and Georgian Bay, and dispatched a troop of men to build a fort at entrance to the St. Clair River (later Fort Gratiot) to prevent British raiders from doing any harm to the American fleet on its way to Lake Huron.

Sinclair was aware of the preciousness of supplies to a campaign in the Northwest. Upon learning of the various gristmills that dotted the Canadian Lake Erie shoreline around Port Dover, he ordered an amphibious raid of about seven hundred men — under Colonel John Campbell of the U.S. 19th Regiment — to destroy them. His purpose was to deny supplies to the British in the Northwest and along the Niagara, and attempt to starve them from the field as Procter had been.[175]

Campbell's raid was devastatingly effective. At four o'clock in the afternoon on 14 May, Campbell landed his troops at the mouth of

Patterson's Creek, near Port Dover. Taking advantage of a heavy fog, the approaching American fleet managed to remain undetected until only an hour before they began to land their soldiers. Colonel Thomas Talbot, the local militia commander, did not have enough time to muster his troops on such short notice. He retreated to Sovereign's Mills, up the Grand River from Port Dover, and mustered what local militia he could collect. He was joined by a detachment of the 19th Light Dragoons, and the next day marched to meet the invaders.[176]

Port Dover had been burnt, along with the local gristmills. As Talbot's troops picked through the wreckage of the little lakeside town, Campbell's troops moved down the lake toward Turkey Point. They burned Finch's mills the next morning, before returning across the lake to Erie. General Drummond was disgusted by this war against food production and supplies. "Every private house, and other building belonging to the peaceable inhabitants of the Village, and neighbourhood of Dover, has been reduced to ashes," he warned Prevost. "And as their Officers appear determined to pursue the same system, throughout the whole of the Western Frontier, I feel convinced, that nothing but the most vigorous opposition to such disgraceful proceedings will prevent a recurrence of them."[177]

* * *

Drummond was born at Quebec in 1772. The son of a merchant with military ties, he had been in the army since he was seventeen. He rose rapidly through the ranks, eventually becoming a lieutenant general in June 1811. He served several garrison posts, including Gibraltar and Ireland besides Canada, and had fought in Holland. In December 1813, the experienced and energetic Drummond was back in Canada, assuming command of the British forces in Upper Canada. That winter he planned several offensives against the Americans, including an aborted plan to destroy the Lake Erie fleet by mounting his men on sleds and crossing the ice. That summer pitted Drummond against the overland prong of the American plan, and he would spend most of 1814 fighting pitched battles along the Niagara frontier.[178]

Sir Gordon Drummond took command of the British military forces in Upper Canada in December 1813. A career army officer, Drummond brought energy and professionalism to his command. Reporting to Sir George Prevost, Drummond commanded the British forces at the famous battle of Lundy's Lane and directed the siege of Fort Erie in 1814. ("Sir Gordon Drummond," artist Charles William Jefferys / Library and Archives Canada / C-70394)

Drummond was not the only one disgusted by Campbell's raid. While Sinclair and the United States government approved of the burning of military targets such as gristmills, they disavowed his destruction of civilian homes. Sinclair wrote to the Secretary of the Navy, "I am sorry to learn that several private houses were also destroyed, which was so contrary to my wish, and to the idea I have of our true policy to those people [of Upper Canada]."[179] Campbell was court-martialed, and was later killed at the Battle of Chippawa on the Niagara frontier.[180]

While Sinclair was new to Lake Erie, he wasted no time in becoming familiar with the situation on that lake. He employed an Upper Canadian traitor, Abraham Markle, to keep him informed of British military operations. Markle had been a prominent member of Upper Canadian society. A wealthy miller, distiller and landowner, he had spent the first year of the war peacefully. In 1813, however, several complaints — which called Markle's loyalty into question — were made to the British commander.[181] After spending some time in prison, Markle joined the Canadian Volunteers, an American army unit made up of expatriate Upper Canadians.

Markle ran a spy ring in Upper Canada. With complete command of Lake Erie, Sinclair was able to put Markle and his men ashore, where they travelled to various British military posts and gathered information. Markle's intelligence network was vast. His spies made contact with American sympathizers in Upper Canada, who fed information back to the Americans. The wives of some of the sympathizers befriended the wives of senior British military officers and reported the gossip back to Markle. Several times, Sinclair dropped Markle off on the Upper Canadian shore, and each time he was picked up, Markle had new information on the British.

One of Markle's spies made it to York, where he heard rumours that the British were building boats on Lake Huron. A thousand men, Markle said, were travelling by way of Lake Simcoe with all kinds of building supplies and cannon. "Indeed," Sinclair reported to his superiors, "no undertaking of theirs during the war has been kept so profound a secret as has this."[182] Sinclair, greatly aided by Markle's intelligence activities, knew that he must try and destroy the British naval base on Lake Huron, or face a new British fleet on the upper Great Lakes. For a new commander, Sinclair was showing great flair for strategic thought and mastery.

The Americans were not alone in assigning a new commander to the upper Great Lakes. Lieutenant Miller Worsley of the Royal Navy was selected to relieve Poyntz and take command of Lake Huron. With an additional handful of seamen, he was to reinforce the isolated post and take command of the few British boats left on Lake Huron. In response to McDouall's complaints about Poyntz, Sir James Yeo gave his young lieutenant extra instructions. "It is my most positive orders and directions, that you comply with all requisitions made to you from time to time by L. Colonel McDouall or the officer commanding the Military Post at Michilimackinac."[183] With these explicit instructions to co-operate, Worsley was off on his first independent command.

Worsley was a young and eager naval officer. He had made lieutenant the year before and had served aboard several of the British vessels on Lake Ontario in 1813. As a midshipman, Worsley had served aboard the *Swiftsure* with Robert Barclay when the latter was a lieutenant, and had fought in the battle of Trafalgar. With his fresh new posting, Worsley hoped to impress his superior officers and to further his career.

In July, Worsley made the overland journey from the base at Kingston to the Nottawasaga River. There, with another reinforcement draft of sailors, and Assistant Surgeon James Samson of the Royal Newfoundland Regiment, he waited for the *Nancy* to arrive on her next supply run. They were kept waiting about a week, "during which time we suffered every misery that you can imagine from bad weather and myriads of musquettos," complained one of Worsley's companions. It was an uncomfortable week for Worsley and his crew. Apart from swarms of mosquitoes and rain, the little band also had to contend with some friction with a local band of Natives, who periodically snuck into the sailors' wigwams. The Nottawasaga River was also not the most ideal camping spot. "The land here is the most barren I have seen and seems to have been formed from time to time by the washing of Lake Huron, it being for upward two miles composed entirely of banks of sand, on which nothing grows but small brush wood."[184] The *Nancy* arrived off the river entrance on 2 August and came safely to the wharf — all to the great relief and expectation of Worsley's little band.

With the *Nancy* at the Nottawasaga, Worsley replaced Poyntz and work immediately began to load her with more supplies for Michilimackinac. The logistics of moving supplies from York and down the Nottawasaga River had improved since the *Nancy*'s last run, and this time Worsley was able to stow 157 barrels of flour, 143 barrels of pork, six barrels of salt, and over 100 pairs of shoes.[185] Packed tightly with these badly needed provisions, the *Nancy* set sail for Michilimackinac.

Arthur Sinclair and the Erie fleet were not the only threats to the Northwest, however. That spring, McDouall learned that a contingent of Americans had floated up the Mississippi River to Prairie du Chien, in modern-day Wisconsin. The Mississippi River route was an old fur-trade highway, and through Lake Michigan the fur traders at Michilimackinac had been able to establish a firm business relationship with the various Native nations south and west of the lake. Sioux, Winnebagos and others all used the Prairie du Chien trading post to receive gifts from the British Indian Department and to trade for goods.[186]

It was from this post that many of the warriors who had gone to capture Michilimackinac, Detroit and others had congregated and begun their journey. Many had familial or national connections to the area, and the presence of a large American force was prompting many of McDouall's Native allies to worry about the safety of their kin. When rumours began to float upriver of American atrocities, McDouall's Native allies began screaming for revenge. McDouall himself was sympathetic to their concerns; he, too, was worried about the broader strategic implications of American possession of the Mississippi. "Nothing could then prevent the Enemy from gaining the Source of the Mississippi, gradually extending themselves by the Red River to Lake Winnipic from whence the descent of Nelsons River to York Fort would in time be easy," McDouall explained to Drummond. "The total subjugation of the Indians on the Mississippi would either lead to their extermination by the enemy or they would be spared on the express condition of assisting them to expel us from Upper Canada."[187] The loss of Prairie du Chien could mean the loss of Mackinac, the Northwest, and eventually Upper Canada. McDouall had to do something, so he called on the North West Company.

* * *

Major William McKay had been an employee of the company for some time. As its agent, he had travelled many of the waterways branching from the upper Great Lakes and was not only familiar with many of the Native nations and languages, but was also popular with those people. McDouall promoted the ex-Nor'Wester to the rank of lieutenant colonel and placed him in charge of a force of seventy-five North West Company militia and the 136 warriors he could spare from Michilimakinac. McDouall also gave him a small three-pounder field gun, much to the satisfaction of the Native chiefs. On 28 June, McKay and his army set out from Mackinac and headed for the Mississippi to secure the back door to the Canadian Northwest.

On 17 July, McKay and his expeditionary force reached Prairie du Chien. Along the way, more Native warriors had joined his force, eager to have a part in pushing the Americans from their territory. By the time McKay's army reached the Mississippi, he was in command of 650 men.[188] He needed them all: the Americans had built a little fort with two strong blockhouses and six cannon manned by sixty men; in the river was a gunboat bristling with fourteen cannon and an additional seventy men. It was a strong position, and McKay would have to make full use of his resources to take it.

After sending the traditional demand to surrender, McKay set up his one cannon and began firing at the fort and the gunboat. His men did well, with two-thirds of the shots smashing into the gunboat. The little three-pounder's shot was so effective that, after three hours of battering, the gunboat was forced to cut its cable and head downriver and out of range. McKay did not let the gunboat go so easily. He sent a detachment of two dozen militia and some local Sauk warriors in pursuit. They caught up to the gunboat downstream, but there was another gunboat lying in wait there. With only small arms, the Canadian militia attacked, but could not capture, the boats. Instead, the Americans weighed their anchors and went even further downstream. The militia, having done everything it thought possible, returned to the fort, leaving the Sauks to watch the river. The Sauk warriors waited patiently, and were rewarded three days later when six American supply barges, armed and ready for battle, arrived upriver. On the morning of 22 July, all the available Sauks, including women, mustered together and attacked the boats. They captured one boat, including its cannon, and forced the rest to retreat.[189]

The attack on Prairie du Chien, meanwhile, was turning into a siege. McKay and his gunners, with warm hearts and high expectations, kept up the bombardment of the fort for a day and half, while his accompanying Native warriors had ringed the fort and kept up a constant clatter of small-arms fire. The blockhouses were too strong, and McKay found that not only was the fire of his Native allies useless, but that his little three-pounder was equally ineffective. To make matters worse, he was running out of ammunition for his cannon. By 19 July he had "Only Six rounds round Shott remaining including three of the Enemies we had picked up."[190] He prepared two breastworks, one at 700 yards from the fort, the other at 450. McKay hoped to heat the last of his ammunition red hot and set the blockhouses on fire.

Just as the first hot shot was being loaded into the three-pounder, a white flag was draped out of the fort. The American commander, hoping to spare his men from a massacre, offered his surrender. McKay jumped at the chance, and immediately took control of the fort's cannon. The next day the Americans formally marched out of the fort and surrendered. Afraid that the American prisoners would eat too large a portion of his supplies, and that their presence might incite the Natives, McKay ordered them transported to St. Louis and sent word of his victory back to McDouall. The old Nor'Wester had secured the western approaches to Michilimackinac, and, temporarily at least, kept the Northwest for Canada.

Sinclair, meanwhile, was busy on Lake Erie, preparing to undo McKay's work. He wasted little time in executing his orders to capture the British Northwest. Hidden somewhere among Georgian Bay's rocky islands and mysterious fogbanks, Sinclair knew, was the growing British supply depot and shipbuilding yard at Matchedash Bay. The Americans, through their spy networks, had heard vague and varied reports about Matchedash for some time, and Sinclair wanted to erase all possibility of it being used to succor the fort at Michilimackinac before he attacked it. The fleet spent some time poking around the various islands and cautiously probing the dangerous channels before finally giving up. The uncharted waters served as an

Fort St. Joseph on an island of the same name, at the northern rim of Lake Huron, served as the staging ground for the British forces that captured Michilimackinac on 17 July 1812. With the Treaty of Ghent, Michilimackinac returned to American hands. Following the war, the British abandoned their former post on St. Joseph's Island in favour of a more accessible and comfortable location on nearby Drummond Island. ("Fort St. Joseph," artist Edward Walsh / William L. Clements Library)

impenetrable barrier, and with the summer wearing on, Sinclair headed for his other objectives.[191]

Next, he steered the fleet to St. Joseph's Island — and, to his disappointment, found the post abandoned. The British had vanished. Nevertheless, he burned what was left of the blockhouse and stockade, and continued on to the North West Company post at Sault Ste. Marie. On his way there he intercepted the *Mink*, which had been loaded with flour and was on its way back to Sault Ste. Marie. Sinclair then detached several boats, loaded with soldiers under the command of Major Andrew Holmes, and sent them to the North West Company post at Sault Ste. Marie, where *Nancy* and her crew had spent the previous winter.

When the American launches, packed with sailors and soldiers, arrived at the post, they found another supply ship, *Perseverance*, moored on the Lake Superior side of the falls. Despite being badly burned by the evacuating Nor'Westers, Sinclair's detachment managed to pull her over the falls before it succumbed to Lake Huron and sank. For good measure, Sinclair's troops also razed the North West Company's storehouses. Later, Sinclair bragged to his friend in Virginia that the destruction of Sault Ste. Marie had given him complete command of Lake Superior. "I should have branched off upon the advantage that it offered, and ruined the British North West Company," he wrote. "I am well assured that I could have taken Fort William and property contained there to the amount of two millions of Dollars, which would have had a better effect on the Indians than the capture of Mackinack."[192] Fortunately for the North West Company, Sinclair did not try to get creative on the largest of the freshwater lakes. While it is doubtful he could have organized his force to find and destroy Fort William on such a large body of unknown water, his sentiments underline the animosity with which the Americans viewed the North West Company's participation in the war, and the company's value to the British.

Sinclair's raids on St. Joseph's and Sault Ste. Marie left Michilimackinac even more isolated. The only remaining supply depots on Lake Huron were the nascent establishment at Penetanguishene on Georgian Bay, and the more firmly established route via the Nottawasaga. With his powerful fleet, Sinclair could easily blockade Mackinac Island. He and Croghan took the time afforded to them by the power of their position. They arrived at Michilmackinac on 26 July, but over the next week they carefully plotted out the British defences and weighed their options before deciding to attack.

McDouall had not been idle while in command, having strengthened the island's defences. He built an extra blockhouse on the heights above the old fort and made sure he commanded the more open approaches to the British position. The American ships could not elevate their guns enough to hit the new fortifications, and decided to land their army at the farther end of the island. The plan was to build a small fort themselves, and then use their superior numbers to beat McDouall in the woods.[193]

On 4 August, the Americans made their attack. After allotting men to the cannon, McDouall only had around 140 men to repulse the American landing. The area where the American fleet had obviously chosen to drop off the troops included a large cleared area bordered by woods. It was in this clearing that the Americans planned to build their own fort on Mackinac, and where McDouall planned to cut them down with fire from the woods. He ranged his men along the wooded borders of a cleared area, and placed his Native reinforcements along his flanks to channel the Americans into the open field. He also had one six-pound and one three-pound field piece, but he did not have an artillery officer to command them. His men would have to do their best in using the guns.[194]

Sinclair's flotilla bombarded the beach and covered the landing of Croghan's troops. When the Americans began the advance, the two British field pieces "opened a heavy fire upon them, but not with the effect they should have had, being not well manned."[195] The Americans shied away from the open ground, denying McDouall's men the easy shoot they had hoped for. Instead, they began to gradually infiltrate the woods, and they pushed the Natives back on both of McDouall's flanks. He sent detachments of the Michigan Fencibles, a militia regiment made up of men of the North West Company, to shore up his shrinking wings. As he did so, news reached him that an American force had landed behind his left flank, and McDouall took some Natives and fifty militiamen to meet them.

There, the Mackinac defenders made a stand and drove the Americans from the woods. "I again advanced to support a party of the Fallsovine Indians, who with their gallant Chief Thomas had commenced a spirited attack upon the Enemy, who in a short time lost their second in Command and several other Officers," McDouall gleefully reported. "The Enemy retired in the utmost haste and confusion followed by the Troops, 'till they found shelter under the very Broadside of their Ships anchored within a few yards of the shore."[196] The American attack disintegrated with the loss of their officers. With confusion on the field and at the landing point, Croghan called off the attack and ordered the men back to the boats. With losses that totalled thirteen killed and forty-six wounded, the American commanders were forced to reconsider their plans.[197]

When the Americans re-embarked on the ships, Sinclair became convinced that Michilimackinac was an impregnable fortress, one that could not be taken by direct assault. On Lake Erie, Sinclair demonstrated that he understood how fundamental supply routes were to frontier warfare by ordering the attack on Port Dover. After the attack on Michilimackinac failed, he and Croghan decided to put the same principles in action on Lake Huron. Mackinac could be taken more easily, he reasoned, if it were starved a little first. The fleet weighed anchor.

The American militia, as well as the brig *Lawrence* and the schooners *Caledonia* and the captured *Mink,* were sent back to Detroit along with two companies of regular soldiers and all the American militia. Sinclair headed for Georgian Bay with the *Niagara, Scorpion* and *Tigress* and three companies of regular soldiers. He knew that the British were using the Nottawasaga River as a supply point for Michilimackinac, and unlike Matchedash, he knew how to find the Nottawasaga. What he did not know was that the *Nancy* was at the river, waiting to make her final stand.

As the battle had raged around Michilimackinac, the *Nancy* had unknowingly been busy readying for the 220-mile voyage northwest to the island, its hold stuffed with vital provisions for the garrison. McDouall, concerned that his only supply ship might be caught by the American squadron, sent a brave man named Robert Livingston to warn the incoming *Nancy*. Livingston's own account of his service — he is truly one of the walking wounded — is given below in Appendix D.

Livingston had experienced much of the fighting in Northwest. Prior to the war, he had been a North West Company fur trader living on St. Joseph's Island. When Captain Roberts began collecting his army for the attack on Michilimakinac, Livingston convinced thirty-six other

MACKINACK, FROM ROUND ISLAND.[4]

This drawing shows the imposing position of Fort Michilimackinac. Located atop a cliff, the fort dominated the village and wharfs below. In 1814 Sinclair discovered that, lacking howitzers, he could not elevate his naval guns high enough to bombard the fort. Accordingly, he landed his forces on the far side of the island and hoped to beat the British in the open. The plan failed, and the British retained control of Michilmackinac until the end of the war. ("Mackinac from Round Island," artist unknown / Library and Archives Canada / C-015127) men to join him. The number was enough to get Livingston a commission in the British Indian Department, and as such he served as a guide, courier, interpreter and liaison with the Native tribes of the upper Great lakes. He had been captured twice by the Americans, had taken a tomahawk in his right eye, had been four times severely wounded, especially to a leg and shoulder, and had served from Michilimackinac to Detroit to the Niagara Peninsula. He carried a musket ball, still unextracted, in his right thigh, and had use of one eye and one arm. In the spring he had guided the *Nancy* on her first voyage to the Nottawasaga. Now, with the American fleet lying in wait, Livingston once again journeyed for his country. He set out in an open canoe and passed unnoticed through the line of American ships. From there he paddled out into the open waters of Lake Huron, where he hoped to intercept the *Nancy*.[198]

Livingston caught the *Nancy* only a few hours' sail from the Nottawasaga River.[199] He delivered the warning of the American fleet, and relayed instructions from McDouall. The *Nancy* was to return to the Nottawasaga, where she and her crew were to fortify themselves against an American attack. For the benefit of the sailors, the seasoned soldier McDouall included some helpful hints for building fortifications. They were to construct a strong blockhouse "with Loop Holes and Embrasures for your two six pounders."[200] There, Worsley was to guard the provisions he had with him, and possibly forward them later on in smaller bateaux armed with the *Nancy*'s carronades. Even with the threat of an American assault on Michilimackinac, McDouall was organizing the future resupply of the island. He had arranged for future supplies to be brought by bateaux to secret storage areas on the Sauganock and Thessalon rivers, where he hoped he could amass enough supplies using canoes and bateaux to keep him over the winter.[201] Worsley immediately put the *Nancy*'s helm about and steered back to the Nottawasaga.

The Nottawasaga River bends shortly before reaching Lake Huron, creating a long, narrow peninsula between the river and Lake. It was behind this scrubby, sandy peninsula that Worsley hid the *Nancy*, about two miles from the river's mouth.

Livingston left immediately. He was carrying dispatches from McDouall to Drummond, which explained the dire situation

After the American victory at Moraviantown on 5 October 1813, the Nottawasaga River became the primary British supply route to Michilimackinac. Here the *Nancy* fought her fiery final battle. Near its mouth, the Nottawasaga River is divided from Lake Huron by a long stretch of rolling sand dunes. This is how the Nottawasaga appeared in the early nineteenth century, not too long after the battle. The tall trees and high sandy banks, clearly visible in the print, served to hide and protect the *Nancy* from American cannon fire. ("Mouth of Nottawasaga," artist Alexander Cavalié Mercer / Library and Archives Canada / C-035939)

Michilimackinac faced. Livingston headed up the Nottawasaga to Lake Simcoe, and from there to York. From York, a courier could run the dispatches to Drummond, who was overseeing the siege of Fort Erie on the Niagara Peninsula. Knowing that Worsley needed all the men he could get, Livingston immediately returned to the Nottawasaga after seeing the letters off. When Drummond read of the danger to the *Nancy*, he flew into action. Militia detachments and Native warriors were ordered to head immediately for the Nottawasaga to protect the little schooner in her vulnerable anchorage.[202] The reinforcements would take time to get to the *Nancy*, however, and with Sinclair's fleet prowling Georgian Bay, time was not on the British side.

While Livingston was away, Worsley prepared for battle. The *Nancy*'s three small guns were hoisted out and put on shore. On the southeast bank of the river, Worsley and his men built a small, stout blockhouse. It was placed so as to afford protection to the *Nancy* lying below it, and was suitably protected from the lake by a row of sand dunes. The cannon were mounted in the embrasures of the blockhouse or on the ground, and powder and ammunition stockpiled in readiness.[203] When Livingston returned, he rounded up twenty-three willing Native warriors from Nottawasaga to help in the defence of the little schooner.

For the defence, Worsley had twenty seamen and Newfoundlanders, nine Canadians and twenty-one Natives; Livingston had twenty-three Natives, for a grand total of seventy-five. Against them, in attack, was a U.S. naval and army force of 380. The number of cannon and small arms was pathetic on the Imperial side when compared against U.S. figures.

The defenders did not have to wait long. On 13 August, Sinclair arrived from his expedition to Matchedash. He had with him the *Niagara*, *Tigress* and *Scorpion*, and besides his sailors and marines, a force of over four hundred soldiers. The *Niagara* still had its eighteen 32-pounder carronades and two long 12-pounders. The *Tigress* and *Scorpion* each had a long 24-pounder gun. The *Scorpion* carried an additional 12-pounder and Croghan's troops had two small field howitzers with them.

For Worsley and his men, the situation looked grim. They were obviously heavily outgunned and outnumbered. It is doubtful Worsley knew that Drummond's reinforcements were on their way, and even if he did, the matter was moot. All Worsley had to defend his little schooner

Once Lieutenant Miller Worsley learned that an American squadron, under the command of Arthur Sinclair, had crossed into Lake Huron, he hid the *Nancy* one mile up the Nottawasaga River. Worsley built a blockhouse atop one of the tall riverbanks to protect his little schooner. On 14 August 1814, Sinclair found the *Nancy*, and began to bombard Worsley's position. After a day-long fight, Worsley blew up the *Nancy* and his blockhouse and retreated up the river. The remains of the *Nancy* sank under the waters of the Nottawasaga. For years after the War of 1812 this small pile of rubble on the river bank was the only evidence of the battle. ("Remains of Lt. Worsley's Blockhouse," artist Alexander Cavalié Mercer / Library and Archives Canada / C-018280)

were his sailors and a few local Natives. Nonetheless, he and his men prepared to stand their ground and defend the *Nancy*. At nine o'clock in the morning, tongues of fire and smoke burst from the U.S. naval guns, red-hot shot flying in long shallow arcs in quest of known targets.

After the surprises at Michilimackinac, Croghan was more cautious in his approach to the Nottawasaga supply depot. He landed a reconnaissance party on shore, which slowly penetrated the woods to the British position. They returned, and they reported the presence of the *Nancy* in the river, and of the blockhouse. It was too late in the day to mount a concentrated attack, so the Americans waited until the next day.[204] At nine o'clock in the morning on 14 August, Sinclair's flotilla stood into range, anchored within good battering range, and began the bombardment. The *Nancy*'s defenders did what they could in reply, and soon the Americans became frustrated. Worsley's blockhouse was in a good position, hidden by sand hills and trees that frequently interrupted Sinclair's shot. Despite the vast disparity between the two forces, his little band of sailors, Natives and Mackintosh's North West Company men held their own. As the morning turned into afternoon, the artillery duel began to look like a stalemate. Even so, these were desperate hours ashore.

Sinclair was not a man to be stopped so easily. He mounted both of the army's howitzers into a launch and sent them to Croghan's men on the shore. From there, the American soldiers could refresh the attack on the blockhouse by bombarding from the land. The tide was about to turn. Soon, Worsley's position was under fire from two sides. The blockhouse and the *Nancy*, Worsley and his men, were subjected to heavy pounding. It was an untenable position. Outnumbered, outgunned and "finding my little crew were falling all round me,"[205] Worsley decided that the end had come.

He gave orders to prepare the schooner for demolition. As Mackintosh had decided in the St. Clair River, the *Nancy* was too valuable a prize to be handed to the Americans. The powder was set, the wounded collected, and the guns in the blockhouse were spiked. At four o'clock in the afternoon, with the withering shot raining down on them, the fire was put to the *Nancy* and she went up in smoke. The blockhouse, linked to the *Nancy* by a powder train, also flashed into flame.

The explosion of the blockhouse and the fire in the *Nancy* startled Croghan's men. From the ship, Sinclair thought that one of the shells from the howitzer had ignited the blockhouse's powder magazine and set off a powder train to the *Nancy*. When they had recovered from the shock, the American commander on shore ordered his men to try and board the *Nancy* and extinguish the flames, "but frequent and heavy explosions below deck made the risque of lives too great to attempt saving her — she was therefore, with her valuable Cargo, entirely consumed."[206] In all the confusion, Worsley had perfect cover for his next move. He and his men, carrying what they could — small arms, personal effects and provisions — slipped quickly out into the woods, unnoticed by the American forces pouring ashore.

After seven hours of fighting, the battle was over. Elated that he had swept the last remaining British vessel from the upper Great Lakes, Sinclair detached two schooners to Lake Huron and triumphantly headed back to Lake Erie with the rest of his fleet. Sinclair was confident that by blocking the Nottawasaga, no large supply shipments could reach Michilimackinac. Without these, Sinclair was confident, the British post would starve. The next spring, McDouall would be in no position to offer a stiff resistance. One way or another, the Northwest would be American.[207]

Lieutenant Daniel Turner, in overall command of the *Scorpion* and the *Tigress*, was ordered to blockade the mouth of the Nottawasaga and prevent further supplies from reaching Michilimackinac. Turner did as he was told, and rode out a Lake Huron storm in the lee of two small islands off the mouth of the Nottawasaga. It was the kind of storm that had battered the *Nancy* the previous fall. The Americans were learning first-hand what kind of weather the upper lakes could throw at a wooden vessel. Turner had trouble keeping his two schooners on station in such weather, and the fear of being blown against the shoreline frequently crept into the minds of Turner's officers. After enduring three storms off the mouth of the Nottawasaga, Turner decided to head north.

Sinclair's instructions to Turner had allowed him the option of detaching one of the schooners to cruise off St. Joseph's and cut the fur-trade route between Michilimackinac and the French River. Sinclair reasoned that only one of his powerful Erie-built schooners would be enough to stop any supply mission that ventured out of the Nottawasaga. Severing the French River route would put additional pressure on Michilimackinac and worsen the British supply situation. The Nottawasaga was the priority, however, and Sinclair expressly told his subordinate to watch it at all costs, and to be wary of the British. Sinclair did not trust Worsley's retreat, and ordered Turner to make sure all shore parties were closely guarded and kept under the cover of the schooner's guns. He also warned him against surprise attacks.[208]

Despite his orders, Turner turned the two schooners toward St. Joseph's. He reasoned that the two vessels would be able to choke all traffic between Michilimackinac and both the Nottawasaga and French rivers. Michilimackinac would be completely isolated if he could keep up the blockade until October, when the weather would make it impossible to reinforce McDouall anyway. So it was that the *Scorpion* and the *Tigress* weighed anchor and left the scene of the *Nancy*'s final battle. So it was they went to cut off the French River route, the only way left to Mackinac.

5

Worsley's War

With the smoke of the smouldering *Nancy* still rising behind them and with gathering darkness offering desperately needed cover, Miller Worsley and his men probed their way through thick woods and up river. It was tough going. They had to carry several wounded men, and soon they were discarding any articles too awkward or heavy to carry. For instance, Worsley's precious desk, which contained several letters and militarily sensitive dispatches, was left by the side of the river. Robert Livingston's Native friends lurked in the woods as a rearguard, firing at the American landing parties and wounding one American soldier to cover the British escape.[209]

The Nottawasaga, a narrow, densely wooded stream, snaked its way through hard, rocky country. Its use as a supply route reflected a strategic, military need, and it had no farms, towns or other civilized elements along its banks. For thirty-six miles, following an Iroquois trail, Worsley led his band through the mosquito-infested forest, before finally spotting a little cabin where he could comfortably rest his wounded. Assistant Surgeon Sampson did his best for the wounded men. One sailor had been hit in the arm; the bone had been completely shattered, but Sampson managed to conduct a full amputation with no complications. The sailor lived, and made a full recovery.[210]

It was dark and hot and his men were exhausted. Worsley had not only lost his first command, but had lost all of his own personal possessions —

and those of his men. As Worsley later wrote to his father, "We lost everything we had except what we stood upright in."[211] The little house they reached that night was in fact Fort Willow, the palisaded supply depot at the head of the Nottawasaga and the marshalling point for goods arriving overland from Lake Simcoe and heading to Michilimackinac. There his men could rest and recuperate among the barrels and boxes labelled for the Northwest — items which could not now reach the stretched troops at Michilimackinac.

For two days, the little band rested at Fort Willow. With the *Nancy* now destroyed, Lieutenant Colonel Robert McDouall's plans to transfer the crew of the *Nancy* to bateaux and bring provisions up to the secret inlets near Micilimackinac could still be carried out, and without any worry of having to guard the vessel. But Worsley still needed time. The Americans were most likely still at the mouth of the Nottawasaga, and the necessary provisions and supplies needed to be organized. After two days at Fort Willow, Worsley began loading provisions into the bateaux on the Nottawasaga River.

In total, he had the equivalent of sixty-seven barrels of flour and three barrels of pork with him,[212] and with eighteen men he set out in two open boats, along with one canoe piloted by Livingston. The little band made the run back down the Nottawasaga to their former battleground, where they discovered the Americans had felled trees across the river to prevent more supply boats from reaching Lake Huron. After expending some effort, they managed to clear the obstruction. They then began the 380-mile marathon paddle up the western edge of Georgian Bay. They made the trip in six days, skirting the rocky coast and heading for the channel on the north side of Manitoulin Island called the Detour. Livingston, the dedicated fur trader and vastly experienced water traveller, showed them the way. They had safely got to within forty miles of Michilimackinac, when to Worsley's horror they found the *Tigress* and the *Scorpion* riding at anchor in the narrow Detour.[213]

The two gunboats had become impatient with the blockade of the swampy river. Lieutenant Daniel Turner, in command of both American schooners, could not find a decent anchorage, and after three powerful Lake Huron gales he worried that his exposed ships might be dashed to splinters on the granite shore of Georgian Bay. After only a short time, he led *Scorpion* and *Tigress* north, to the safer waters of the Detour and the greater possibility of intercepting British canoes from the French River.[214] They were not there long before Worsley's two boats caught sight of them. The British quickly put into a little bay and hid out of sight of the American gunboats until night fell. Then they exchanged their boats for canoes and quietly slipped past the blockading vessels in the darkness.[215]

The sailors arrived at Michilimackinac the next day, and Worsley explained the situation to McDouall. McDouall had already received a report from several Natives that there were American ships in the Detour; now he listened with great interest as Worsley not only confirmed the report, but also eagerly proposed that "they might be attacked with every prospect of success."[216] The way to the French River and Georgian Bay must be opened for Michilimackinac to survive, and this meant removing the American gunboats. McDouall quickly agreed to the expedition, and offered Worsley the services of the Royal Newfoundland Regiment. Worsley was teamed with Lieutenant Andrew H. Bulger of the Royal Newfoundland Regiment, and as co-commanders of the expedition, the two massed their forces.

They were to have four boats, one full of Worsley's Royal Navy sailors, the other three crammed with the Newfoundlanders the *Nancy* had ferried to Michilmackinac that spring. Two of the boats were outfitted with small cannon, not much of an armament against two strong schooners of the U.S. Navy. But on the British side fortunes ran high, and it was known that fortune favoured the brave. On 1 September Worsley, Bulger, their troops and an escort of Native warriors defiantly set out to clear the lake of Americans. The next day, they camped near the Detour. On the morning of 3 September Worsley, ever the enterprising officer, left the main body of his troops and sailors ashore and set out in a canoe, "for the purpose of reconnoitering the Enemy's position, being fearful that they might have shifted it during my absence."[217] Worsley found the *Tigress* anchored about six miles away, but no sign of the *Scorpion*. With the *Tigress* alone and vulnerable, Worsley was determined to take her that night. At six o'clock on the evening of 3 September, Worsley and Bulger left their Native escort behind, and the professional soldiers and sailors rowed out to take the

American. By nine o'clock they were within range of the gunboat. The September night and muffled oars had cloaked their progress, and it was only when the four boats were within ten yards that the American watchmen noticed them. They hailed, hoping that Worsley and Bulger's force was friendly. The British did not bother to give a reply, and the *Tigress* opened fire.

Worsley's boatload of sailors, and a Newfoundland boat under the command of Lieutenant Alfred Armstrong, climbed the *Tigress*'s starboard side. Lieutenant Bulger's boat and that of Lieutenant John Radenhurst attacked the port side. The men of the *Tigress* fired their large twenty-four-pounder gun, but they missed the incoming British boats. With British soldiers and seamen swarming both sides of the schooner, the Americans desperately tried to use their small arms, but with little effect. Against Worsley's well-coordinated attack, the Americans stood little chance.[218]

Three American sailors were killed and thrown overboard; three more were wounded, as were all the officers. The thirty crew members were quickly overwhelmed and forced below, and the *Tigress* became British with minimal losses to the men from Michilimackinac. Two of Worsley's seamen were killed, and two wounded. Lieutenant Bulger and seven men of the Royal Newfoundland Regiment were wounded.[219] With one American vessel captured, there was only one more to go and the British would be back in control of Lake Huron.

Early the next morning, the American prisoners were sent to Michilimackinac under guard. The Americans had informed their captors that the *Scorpion* was only about fifteen miles away. With the prisoners paddling safely off in the distance, Worsley and Bulger prepared to meet the second American gunboat. The intrepid Livingston set out in his canoe to find it; he returned after two hours and informed Worsley that the *Scorpion* was slowly making its way toward the *Tigress*. As Worsley later reported, "I knew from the distance [*Scorpion*] must have been off, that they could not have heard the firing, and consequently must have been ignorant of her consort's having been captured."[220]

To lull the second American gunboat into a sense of security, Worsley kept the American flag flying at the *Tigress*'s masthead. Some of Bulger's troops donned great coats to cover their scarlet uniforms, while the rest found ways of secreting themselves beneath the decks of the *Tigress*, just out of sight, but from points where they could easily rush to attack the second American vessel. On 5 September the *Scorpion*, commanded by Turner, finally made its appearance and leisurely anchored two miles from *Tigress*. Worsley's ruse worked: Turner suspected nothing. Bulger had hidden most of the Newfoundlanders below decks and the rest were lying down to avoid detection. As day dawned on 6 September, the Americans were still unaware that the *Tigress* was officered and manned by the enemy.

With the growing daylight, Worsley made his move. Under only a jib and a foresail, the *Tigress* bore down on the unsuspecting *Scorpion*. Within moments she was alongside, but the American crew still had not noticed anything amiss — "So little were they apprehensive of our design that they were employed washing Decks."[221] When he was within twelve yards of the *Scorpion*, Worsley opened fire with the long twenty-four-pounder. Only then did the Americans realize they had been fooled. The gun was the signal to the soldiers, and the men of the Royal Newfoundland Regiment flew out of their hiding places in the hold and in the cabin. The soldiers swiftly fired a volley, and then, accompanied by the sailors, stormed the American's decks. In less than five minutes the sailors and Newfoundlanders were swarming over the *Scorpion*. Caught by surprise, and with five men killed and two wounded, Turner had no option but to surrender. Worsley's revenge was complete. He had avenged the loss of the *Nancy*. Not only had he captured two of the vessels responsible for the destruction of his first command, but he had also reclaimed command of Lake Huron for the British. He and Bulger had secured Michilimackinac and its supply lines for the rest of the season. Out of the demise of the *Nancy* had grown a stronger and more powerful British presence on Lake Huron.

The British were elated with Worsley's success. McDouall heaped praise upon the young lieutenant in his report to General Gordon Drummond: "In calling your attention to the conspicuousment of the officer who so judiciously planned & carried into effect the well concerted enterprize. I am conscious that I only do Lieut. Worsley a strict justice in acknowledging the eminent services which he has rendered this Garrison.... [H]e with his gallant little band of seamen, has traversed this extensive Lake in two boats laden with provisions for the garrison, & having at this extremity of it, discovered two of his former opponents, his active and indefatigable mind rested not, till he had relieved us from such troublesome neighbours and conducted the blockading force in triumph into our Post."[222] Miller Worsley had saved Michilimackinac and the British in the Northwest, and now he was the toast of the north.

With Lake Huron swept of the Americans, supplies could be flooded into the Northwest theatre. On 10 September a large fleet of canoes, loaded with every manner of supply and provisions, left Lachine for Michilimackinac. Twelve days later, a second fleet group, equally crammed with supplies, struck out from Lachine to the Northwest.[223] Had Turner and his gunboats been prowling the mouth of the French River when the two brigades of canoes arrived, the fate of Michilimackinac might have been much as Sinclair had envisaged it. Instead, with the *Tigress* and *Scorpion* under the Union Jack, the war materiel flooded into the British-controlled Northwest.

These supplies were earmarked for the Native nations of the Northwest to keep them fighting against the Americans.[224] By 28 October 1814, Robert Dickson, the senior Indian Agent at Michilimackinac, had a fully stocked magazine. Included in his supplies were more than 5,000 rounds of ammunition, 200 guns, and 3,933 pounds of gunpowder. There were also non-military supplies, including over a thousand blankets and 4,000 pounds of flour.[225] These supplies, like the ones the year before, were quickly loaded onto boats and shipped to Lake Michigan for distribution.

Details of the capture of *Scorpion* and *Tigress* reached Arthur Sinclair a month later, when several of the gunboats' crewmen escaped while being transported as prisoners to Kingston. Sinclair was predictably furious. The "story is a most unfavourable one, and such as I am loath to believe true, from the whole known character of Lieut. Turner," he reported to the Secretary of the Navy. "I had given Lieut. Turner a picked crew from this vessel, with my Sailing Master, and had added to both their crews 25 chosen men borrowed from Col. Croghan, to act as Marines. I had also left him a boarding netting. Indeed there was no precaution I did not take, in anticipation of every effort, I knew the Enemy would make to regain their line of communication on which their very existence depended."[226] In the attacks on both the *Tigress* and the *Scorpion*, neither vessel had been prepared for a cutting-out expedition like the one Worsley and Bulger had mounted. Despite his direct warnings to Turner about just such an eventuality, neither vessel had rigged netting to prevent surprise boardings or worked out a signal system. When they eventually returned to the United States, the commanders of both the *Scorpion* and the *Tigress* were court-martialled for neglect of duty.

Worsley, in the meantime, delighted in his victory. He had not only regained command of Lake Huron, but by taking the *Scorpion* and *Tigress* after losing the *Nancy*, he had effectively doubled the number of vessels under his command. He immediately put the captured American schooners to work, ferrying six months' worth of supplies between the Nottawasaga and Michilimackinac. He also renamed the two gunboats: *Tigress* became, fittingly, *Surprise,* and *Scorpion* became *Confiance.*[227] Two of the Erie boats, which had been carved out of the Pennsylvania wilderness to reclaim the American Northwest, were now property of His Majesty King George. From the cabin of his new flagship, the young Worsley proudly penned a letter to his father detailing his misadventures and adventures on Lake Huron.

With Worsley in control of the water, and his supply lines funnelling everything he needed to his post, McDouall could breathe a little easier. Another American attack had been made up the Mississippi in August, and it had been broken up easily by a war party of Sauks, Winnebagos and Sioux before it reached Prairie du Chien. Now McDouall had the luxury of being able to afford to send a professional military officer to the post. The accomplished Lieutenant Bulger, still smarting from his wound, was given the honour of commanding the back door to Michilimackinac. McDouall had accomplished what he had been charged to do: to keep the Northwest open to the British, their Native allies and the North West Company.

The North West Company had lost all of its major vessels on lakes Huron and Erie during the last two years of the war. In December 1814, it filed a claim with the British authorities to recoup some of that loss. A military board awarded the company £2,200 for loss of the *Nancy*, a further £1,243 for her services, and another £1,000 for loss of the *Mink*. The board was reluctant to decide on compensation for the

Perseverance, since she had not officially been in the British service at the time of loss. In all, then, the North West Company was granted £4,443 as compensation for the service it had rendered the king, as well as for its resulting losses.[228]

To the south, the second prong of the American offensive was stalled. In the spring, General Brown had led a well-trained army across the Niagara River, with the intention of beating the British back to Burlington and isolating York and the Nottawasaga supply line. Drummond, supported by Yeo and the Lake Ontario squadron, met him on the field at Lundy's Lane and forced him to retreat to Fort Erie. There, Drummond kept him bottled up through most of August with a long and bloody siege. That fall, a demoralized American army pulled back across the river to Buffalo. Further east, Chauncey, on Lake Ontario, lost the shipbuilding race. The hundred-gun British ship *Lawrence* tipped the balance of power on that lake in favour of the British. There could be no attack against Kingston without more ships, and Chauncey was forced to wait.

In 1814, the war also came to the United States. Freed from war in Europe, the British Army and the Royal Navy were finally able to send reinforcements to the North American colonies. British squadrons ranged up and down the American coast, choking trade and commerce. A series of amphibious raids were mounted against American coastal communities. Washington was burned. In Quebec, Prevost received thousands of reinforcements from Wellington's army, with whom he was to march down Lake Champlain and attack the American base at Plattsburgh, New York. After massing his troops, Prevost insisted that the small flotilla of Royal Navy vessels on Lake Champlain sail prematurely. In a repetition of the mistakes made on Lake Erie, the British fleet was beaten on Lake Champlain. Prevost immediately called off his own attack and retreated to Montreal.[229]

In the east, the British seized Maine ports and tightened their blockade. In the northeastern states, where support for the war against Britain had never been high, politicians began to seek ways of ending the conflict. In December, a group of New England states sent delegates to a conference in Hartford, Connecticut, where they discussed ways of ending their involvement in the war.[230]

Peace negotiators from both sides had been meeting on and off in Ghent, Belgium, since August 1814. The delegates from both sides came to the table with a long list of grievances, and talks proceeded slowly. The news of the British defeat at Plattsburgh demonstrated that not even Wellington's veterans could break the stalemate in Upper Canada. The war in North America was in a deadlock, and both sides began looking for a honourable way to end the hostilities.

The Treaty of Ghent was signed on Christmas Day 1814, ending the War of 1812. The first article decreed that all borders were to be restored to their pre-war locations. Western Upper Canada was returned to the British, while Michilimackinac, Prairie du Chien, Fort Niagara and the parts of Maine seized by the British were returned to American control. Several boundary commissions were created to finalize some of the unclear delineations made after the American Revolution. The ninth article stipulated that the Americans would not make war on the Natives, and that the British would not encourage the Natives to make war on the Americans. It was the only article that referred to Madison's declared causes for the War of 1812, and was totally unenforceable: there was nothing that could be done to relieve the pressures of American western expansionism, and both parties knew it. The tenth article called for the abolition of slavery, and had nothing whatsoever to do with the war.

News of the peace was slow to reach North America, and even slower to reach the isolated interior, which was frozen in by months of snow and ice. Plans were underway to build two schooners and several gunboats at Matchedash Bay with the idea that they would be ready for hostilities when the ice broke up.[231] They would never see action. While Worsley remained in command on Lake Huron that spring, he was transferred in the summer of 1815 to Lake Ontario, where he commanded the brig HMS *Star* as the opposing fleets were slowly dismantled.[232]

The North West Company was bitterly disappointed with the terms of the treaty. William McGillivray, one of the company's senior partners, wrote to Prevost complaining of the lost territory in Michigan and the upper Mississippi. "The late Treaty bids fair in its consequences to cut off our Intercourse with all the Southern and Western Indians," McGillivray complained, "for the Americans aware (from the circumstances of the

During the War of 1812 the British and Americans competed fiercely to build and maintain the strongest fleets possible. This is an American political cartoon mocking British efforts after the American victory on Lake Champlain on 11 September 1814. Following the War of 1812, the British maintained naval bases on the Great Lakes in case war should again erupt between the two nations. ("John Bull making a new batch of ships to send to the lakes," artist William Charles / Library and Archives Canada / C-132305)

late War) of the influence established by means of the Trade carried on by Canadian Merchants and their Agents resident among the Indians, will naturally use every means to prevent a recurrence of this influence."[233] McGillivray wanted a new fort built as close to Michilimackinac as possible, to secure the Northwest and keep up the fur trade with the Natives of Lake Michigan.

News of the treaty devastated McDouall, who had spent most of 1814 orchestrating the defence of the Northwest. He objected strongly to handing Prairie du Chien over to the Americans, arguing that the local Native tribes had governed the adjacent territory until the Americans attacked it. McDouall suggested that this meant the upper Mississippi should have been handed back to the Sauks, Winnebagos, Sioux and others, not to the Americans. He objected to having to find a new site for a fort, and cynically suggested that the Americans would try and claim any nearby island with any kind of strategic advantage. His most bitter criticism, however, was reserved for the order to give up Michilimackinac itself. He had spent a year making promises to his Native allies, and building an alliance with the Native nations that would help seal the defence of the island. Now, with the word that he would have to give up his post, McDouall became furious:

"The surrender of this most important Island, the key to the whole Western Country, & which they fully expected would have been retained by us, if followed up by that of St. Josephs, and the adjoining Islands, will be to them, such conclusive proofs of our disgrace, & absolute submission to the American Government, that it would be most grossly deceiving ours, to hold forth the expectation of being joined by a single Indian, in the event of another war. — Their neutrality is then, the utmost, perhaps, that we can hope for, & that is more to be desired than expected. Of this be assured, that a more terrible enemy exists not, than a numerous body of Indians, properly managed & led on, in such a Country as Upper Canada."[234]

In the end, Bulger and his men were withdrawn from Prairie du Chien, and McDouall prepared to pack up Mackinac. Prevost ordered that another post be built on St. Joseph's Island, and a substantial naval dockyard at Penetanguishene. Royal Navy ships cruised the lakes for another twenty years, until the expense of maintaining a standing armed fleet exceeded the risk of war. Gradually, relations between Great Britain and the United States relaxed, and gradually the warships disappeared. Many sank at their moorings. With the rise and fall of Penetanguishene, the Nottawasaga was forgotten both as a transportation highway and as a naval post.

The charred bones of the *Nancy* settled to the bottom of the silty Nottawasaga. As the traffic in the waters above her changed from military transports to civilian pleasure craft, the story of the *Nancy* slowly faded from memory. The men who had worked her and fought her dispersed into other areas of life. In the War of 1812 she had participated in many actions, including Hull's invasion of Upper Canada, Procter's battles along the Lake Erie shoreline, and of course the fights for her own life. She had also been instrumental as a transport. It was the men and provisions that she carried which helped direct the war as it was. Supplies to Amherstbug, troops to Sandusky, Bullock to Michilimackinac, and food for the Northwest were all carried below deck and helped shape the outcome of the war.

The struggles for the Northwest and for Michilimackinac are an underrated key to understanding the War of 1812. Conflict in the Northwest helped precipitate the conflict, and stalemate there helped end it. By maintaining Michilimackinac, the British had denied the Americans a strategic door to Upper Canada. They had siphoned American attention and resources away from other theatres of war, and helped leverage an end to what was, for them, a defensive war. The *Nancy*, with her gallant little band of seamen, was an integral part of this defence. As the river's sand built up around her charred ribs, she was eventually buried and forgotten. One hundred years after her last blast of glory, the *Nancy* was entombed in a natural-looking island in the centre of the river.

Finding the Bones of the *Nancy*:
C.H.J. Snider

*T*he Nottawasaga did not cease to be an important military post with the end of the War of 1812. The secret British base at Penetanguishene Bay became an important naval yard on the upper lakes. Even though peace had been arranged between the United States and Great Britain, the one lesson from the war was that communications and supply to the upper lakes were too important to be improvised in a crisis.

At Penetanguishene, the British kept vessels waiting, hoping they would never be needed. Nor did they discard the Nottawasaga. The road from Lake Simcoe to Georgian Bay still needed to be cut, and the route from Lake Simcoe down the Nottawasaga was still found to be as useful as it had been during the war years. Supplies were still forwarded by way of the river, and a small collection of houses and workshops rose near the final resting place of the *Nancy*.[235]

For 113 years the bones of the *Nancy* lay beneath the murky waters of the Nottawasaga River. Local residents of what became known of Wasaga Beach occasionally returned to where the *Nancy* had fought its final battle and found old relics of the last war between Great Britain and the United States. Cannonballs, gunflints, uniform buttons and other historical treasures were picked from the Nottawasaga for years.

One of the most enterprising of souvenir hunters was a man who had himself fought on the *Nancy*. William Wilson was a member of the Royal Navy who had marched overland in 1814 to fight on the freshwater seas. He was among twenty-one British sailors who manned the *Nancy* under Miller Worsley, and he had been there on the hot August day in 1814 when Sinclair's flotilla found the *Nancy* hiding in the Nottawasaga. Following the war, Wilson settled near modern Midland and, as an old sailor often does, began collecting naval memorabilia, artifacts and other items that reminded him of his seafaring days. Among Wilson's collection was the graceful figurehead of the *Nancy*. When the War of 1812 ended and Wilson quit the Royal Navy, he returned to the muddy banks of the Nottawasaga and retrieved the relic, which had been carved for the *Nancy*'s builders in 1789. The figurehead was lost after Wilson's death, but his grandson, Waverly Smith, vividly remembered it hanging in his grandfather's workshop. Based on Smith's recollections, a replica was produced in 1933.[236]

There were other treasure hunters, too, and not all of the nostalgic kind. A story circulated sometime after the war that the *Nancy* had been carrying the pay of the garrison at Michilimackinac. With visions of chests of gold floating in their heads, treasure hunters periodically scoured the woods along the Nottawasaga River's banks, hoping to track down where Worsley and his men might have buried the payroll. All came away empty-handed: there were no chests stuffed with treasure buried among the trees of the Nottawasaga. A review of the *Nancy*'s cargo manifest makes it clear that bullion was not in its hold. Rather, she was stuffed with the necessary articles to feed an army: hundreds of barrels of salt pork and flour, cases of shoes and leather for shoes.[237] For McDouall, the foodstuffs on board represented the real prize. At an isolated outpost at the far end of a tenuous supply system, flour, salted meat and workable leather were all far more valuable than shillings and pennies.

Gradually, however, the story of the *Nancy* began to fade. The treasure hunters gave up, the collectors found new hunting grounds, and the silt of the Nottawasaga River began to slowly bury the remains of the valiant little schooner. By the 1890s, the story was almost completely forgotten.

It was resurrected by that prolific historian of the War of 1812, Ernest Cruikshank. Digging through the National Archives, Cruikshank discovered British military and naval records regarding the wartime service, and loss, of the *Nancy*. In a 1910 article for the Ontario Historical Society entitled "An Episode of the War of 1812: The Story of the Schooner *Nancy*," Cruikshank pieced together the history of the vessel and her vital contribution to the British war in the Northwest.

It was C.H.J. Snider, however, who was to fully revive the story of the old schooner. Snider was an accomplished journalist who was passionate about all things that sailed the Great Lakes. Since his boyhood, he had been drawing and painting ships and sailing the inland seas. As a reporter for the Toronto *Evening Telegram*, he covered the America's Cup race and innumerable other yachting and sailing events. The story of the *Nancy* captured Snider's imagination, and he put his full journalistic talents to the task of finding her.[238]

After extensive research, Snider headed for the Nottawasaga in August 1911. Equipped with diving gear, he dropped into the murky waters of the river and began searching the silted, muddy bottom for the remains of the warrior-schooner. There, almost totally entombed by the river bottom, Snider found the sharp point of a white-oak hull. The *Nancy* had been found again, after nearly a century.

Snider's interest in the *Nancy* only grew deeper after his discovery. In 1913 he published a book about the War of 1812 on the Great Lakes entitled *In the Wake of the Eighteen-Twelvers*. In this book he included a chapter on the *Nancy* and her wartime exploits. The book was written to be enjoyed, and Snider let his imagination mix with thorough research to produce an exciting and dramatic rendition of the *Nancy*'s wartime service. Despite the book's exhilarating narrative, the *Nancy* itself remained hidden beneath the rushing waters of the Nottawasaga.

Snider was not the only man whose imagination was sparked by the story of the *Nancy*. Dr. F.J. Conboy, a Toronto dentist, was vacationing at Wasaga Beach in 1924. He happened to be paddling down the Nottawasaga River one fine summer day when an odd-shaped item sticking out from the riverbank caught his attention. Guiding his canoe over to the object, Conboy reached into the mud and earth and pulled a weighty twenty-four-pound cannonball out from the loose earth. Conboy had read Snider's *In the Wake of the Eighteen-Twelvers* and knew that the remains of the *Nancy* were somewhere close by. For the rest of

The Nottawasaga River probably much as it appeared to Dr. F.J. Conboy, the discoverer of the *Nancy's* remains. In the century following the War of 1812, the Nottawasaga River and the Wasaga beach area became a popular cottage and tourist destination. Here, some of the vacationers can be seen peacefully enjoying their time on the river. In the middle of the river sits Nancy Island, where Conboy unearthed the hull of HMS *Nancy* in 1927. (Photograph courtesy of Rych Mills.)

Water levels on the Great Lakes changed significantly over the years, making the identification of the final resting place of the *Nancy* extremely difficult. In July 1927, after years of unsuccessful searching, Conboy discovered the remains of the *Nancy* near the shore of Nancy Island. Over the summer, a team of volunteers slowly unearthed the *Nancy's* charred timbers. The valiant schooner, lost for over a hundred years, had been found. (Photograph courtesy of Rych Mills.)

the summer, he searched diligently beneath the murky waters of the swirling Nottawasaga.[239]

The river had changed since Snider found the remains of the little fur-trading schooner. Water levels were significantly lower in 1924; the riverbanks had changed, and islands had appeared where none had existed before. The changing geography frustrated Conboy as he tried to retrace Snider's steps and have a look at the *Nancy* for himself.[240]

For two summers, Conboy searched and found nothing. Working up and down the river, he plumbed the depths looking for any signs of the old schooner. He refused to be defeated, instead enlisting the help of local residents who remembered what the river had looked like before the waters had changed, as well as where others had found military artifacts. Working from this information, Conboy retraced his steps and began testing the depths of the Nottawasaga where he thought the *Nancy* must be. But still nothing was found. Then, in July 1927, Conboy was walking along the shore of an innocent-looking island about a mile from the river's mouth. He was looking for a good place to drive a metal stake as part of his search operations when he found what appeared to be a tree root, half-hidden in the muck near the shoreline. Driving his probe into the root, he was alarmed by the sound of metal striking metal. Elated, Conboy realized that he had not found a root, but the very end of a charred piece of white oak.[241] The water levels had dropped so much that the *Nancy* was now no longer on the bottom of the river, but encased in an island.

Working hard, Conboy and some volunteers began gradually to unearth the *Nancy*. Curious cottagers and local residents soon flocked to the scene of the discovery. Old stories about buried treasure circulated through the area, and soon Conboy had more volunteers willing to dig around the *Nancy* than he knew what to do with. As the earth was diligently scraped away from the mud-encased ribs, the *Nancy* saw daylight for the first time in 113 years.[242]

Little items began appearing under the blades of the volunteers' shovels. Cannonballs, musket locks and barrel staves all came into the light. So did evidence of the *Nancy*'s violent end: the wood and metal work looked charred to the volunteers digging her out, and soon they were discovering more items that suggested she went down in a blazing inferno. Musket balls were fused together in large, melted heaps. Pieces

The Raising of the Warship "Nancy", Sept. 1927, Nottawasaga River, Wasaga Beach, Ont.

In September 1927 volunteers raised the remains of the *Nancy* and laid them to rest on Nancy Island, just a short distance from where she had been buried. Local authorities subsequently set up a small museum in her honour. It was the beginnings of the Nancy Island Historic Site. (Photograph courtesy of Rych Mills.)

A variety of museums have housed the remains of the *Nancy* over the years. This picture, from the early 1960s, shows how little of the schooner survived the fire and a century at the bottom of the Nottawasaga. Most recently the remains of the hull rest in a glassed-in and climate controlled exhibit area at Nancy Island Historic Site. (From *HMS Nancy and the War of 1812*, 1963)

of glass, found where Mackintosh's cabin had once been, had been scorched and distorted by some amazing heat.[243]

Although satisfied that he had finally found the remains of the *Nancy*, Conboy became concerned that, left out in the open, the *Nancy* would disintegrate under the enthusiasm of souvenir hunters. He had a member of the provincial police stationed on the island to prevent damage to the historic schooner, and he secured government help in maintaining the security of the site. In 1927 the *Nancy* was pulled from the earth and put on the island a short distance from where she was found.[244]

The next year, a small museum was set up to commemorate the *Nancy* and the War of 1812. The cottagers continued to flock to the long, sandy beach, and the area prospered. Dr. Conboy's interest in the area never waned — he was elected mayor of Wasaga Beach in 1941. C.H.J. Snider's interest continued as well: ever enthusiastic about the schooner, he published *The Story of the "Nancy" and Other Eighteen-Twelvers*, a revised version of his earlier book which included comments on his discovery of the hull. He prepared a report on the *Nancy* for the Archives of Ontario, and in 1936 he reprinted Mackintosh's 1813 log of his voyages in the *Nancy*.

Following the Second World War, the widespread availability of automobiles made the Nottawasaga River and its long, beautiful beach more accessible to tourists. Day trips from Toronto became possible, and little vacation cottages began to spring up around the beach. Meanwhile, interest in local history remained high. In 1955, the Historic Sites and Monument Board of Canada put up a small cairn to commemorate the destruction of the *Nancy* and her heroic final battle. By the 1960s, it was clear that Wasaga Beach was destined to become a tourist haven, and the local chamber of commerce commissioned an archaeological study to help preserve the heritage of the area. In 1962, Dr. Wilfrid Jury of the University of Western Ontario conducted an archaeological survey of the area. Jury had already been involved in digs at Penetanguishene and Fort Willow. He knew the history of the area and was very familiar with the Nottawasaga's importance to the story of the War of 1812. When his survey was complete, he presented numerous artifacts and a three-page report to the chamber of commerce.[245]

The theatre is part of the Nancy Island Historic Site, in Wasaga Beach, Ontario. The museum houses exhibits on the War of 1812 and HMS *Nancy*, as well as the resurrected timbres from the famous schooner. Nancy Island is linked to the mainland by a small footbridge. (From *HMS Nancy and the War of 1812*, 1978)

With as much interest in the *Nancy* and the Nottawasaga as there was, local officials soon realized that they needed help in managing their heritage. The village of Wasaga Beach quickly realized that it had neither the resources nor the expertise to handle the growing influx of tourists into the area, and in 1963 management of the beach was handed over to the provincial government.[246] With its vast resources and abilities, Queen's Park was able to move quickly to protect the memory and artifacts of the *Nancy* and the War of 1812. In 1968 the Museum of the Upper Lakes, which told the story of the gallant little schooner and the other ships of the upper Great Lakes, opened on Nancy Island.

Today, encased behind a protective glass shield, the remains of the *Nancy* are available for the public to view at the Nancy Island Historic Site. Surrounded by artifacts and exhibits that detail her life and journeys, the *Nancy* has taken her place among Canada's best-known sailing vessels. Managed by the energetic staff at Wasaga Beach Provincial Park, the museum is fittingly situated on the island that housed the *Nancy*'s remains for over a hundred years. With the Nottawasaga gurgling past, and with eager schoolchildren curiously examining her charred timbers, the *Nancy* is lost no more, and will never be forgotten.

Postscript

War can bestow a variety of legacies on its heroes. For the men who fought in the War of 1812, life did not end with the signing of the Treaty of Ghent. All moved on to various fates, and while most disappeared from history, some of the principals in the story of the *Nancy* left some trace of their lives after the war.

Alexander Mackintosh returned to Moy, where he and his father rebuilt their shipping business. In 1817 Angus Mackintosh, Alexander's father, bought a new vessel, the 134-ton *Duke of Wellington*, and Alexander became her captain. Economic times were hard after the war, however, and the Mackintoshes were soon engaged in a crippling rate war with other lake transports.[247] In 1827 Alexander's mother died, and he and Angus sold their property, said goodbye to the Great Lakes that had been their lifeblood, and returned to Scotland. When Angus's brother died, Angus became the chieftain of the Mackintosh clan and took up residence at the traditional clan home of Moy Hall.[248] Angus and Alexander had the two brass guns that the *Nancy* had carried with her throughout most of the war sent to Scotland, where they were proudly displayed at Moy. When Angus died in 1833, Alexander became the clan chieftain and lived out his days in Scotland, the memory of desperate days on the lakes frontier fresh in his memory.[249]

Miller Worsley returned to England, and never again saw active service in the Royal Navy. This was not of his doing but a fact of economy. In 1817 he was made inspecting commander of the preventive boats stationed at the Isle of Wight — that is, supervisor of the local coast guard. He married the daughter of a Bristol merchant in 1820 and started a family.[250] In 1831 he unsuccessfully petitioned the king for an active posting in the navy. He died in 1835 at the age of forty-four.

Major General Henry Procter was court-martialled for his actions on the Thames River. He was found guilty on several counts, although he was finally sentenced to a public reprimand because of his years of service. He retired soon after the war. Procter died on 31 October 1822, at the age of fifty-nine.[251]

Lieutenant Colonel Robert McDouall left Canada for Scotland in 1816 on half-pay. The next year he was made a Companion of the Bath. He was eventually promoted to major general in 1841. He died at his home in Scotland in 1848.[252]

General William Henry Harrison, the main antagonist to the *Nancy* and her superiors, found political success in the 1820s, first as a senator and then as ambassador to Colombia. When Democrats regained the White House under Andrew Jackson, however, Harrison fell out of favour. Government appointments went to other people, and by the 1830s the former general of the Army of the Northwest was a clerk in a Cincinnati courthouse.[253] He remained active enough in politics, however, to be on the ballot — with John Tyler as his running mate — in the 1840 presidential election. They won, but the aging Harrison fell ill, and on 4 April 1841 he died, after serving just one month as the president of the United States.

With the return of Michilimackinac to the Americans, the North West Company was once again pushed into trading in the middle ground between the Hudson's Bay Company and the American frontier. Conflict soon arose as the Nor'Westers and the Hudson's Bay employees began competing for furs. Violent clashes soon erupted, culminating at Seven Oaks, the Red River massacre, in 1816. By 1821 the British government was tired of the unruly trade wars, and it forced a merger of the North West and Hudson's Bay Companies. Today the Hudson's Bay Company is one of the largest retailers in Canada.

As to the Great Lakes, inland seas of hot warfare for three fabled years in continental history, they passed slowly out of their armed state of affairs. The arrangement of Anglo-American accord known as the

Rush-Bagot Agreement established levels of naval armament for both sides. Even so, for much of the nineteenth century there were violations to its terms and challenges to the equipoise set in place by its promising and propitious terms. Storm clouds would gather from time to time, threatening this middle ground between Canada and the United States, but the rise of new powers, especially Germany and Japan, would rewrite the New World Order. Canada was never again invaded, and the True North, secured by imperial power as during the War of 1812, gained a new lease on life — and a continental dominion in spite of the United States's power.

Appendix A

"The *Nancy*" by Stan Rogers

The clothes men wear do give them airs, the fellows do compare.
A colonel's regimentals shine, and women call them fair.
I am Alexander MacIntosh, a nephew to the Laird
And I do distain men who are vain, the men with powdered hair.

I command the *Nancy* schooner from the Moy on Lake St. Clair.
On the third day of October, boys, I did set sail from there.
To the garrison at Amherstburg I quickly would repair
With Captain Maxwell and his wife and kids and powdered hair.

Aboard the *Nancy*
In regimentals bright.
Aboard the *Nancy*
With all his pomp and bluster there, aboard the *Nancy*-o.

Below the St. Clair rapids I sent scouts unto the shore
To ask a friendly Wyandotte to say what lay before.
"Amherstburg has fallen, with the same for you in store!
And militia sent to take you there, fifty horse or more."

Up spoke Captain Maxwell then, "Surrender, now, I say!
"Give them your *Nancy* schooner and make off without delay!
"Set me ashore, I do implore. I will not die this way!"
Says I, "You go, or get below, for I'll be on my way!"

Aboard the *Nancy*!
"Surrender, Hell!" I say.
Aboard the *Nancy*
"It's back to Mackinac I'll fight, aboard the *Nancy*-o."

Well up comes Colonel Beaubien, then, who shouts as he comes near.
"Surrender up your schooner and I swear you've naught to fear.
"We've got your Captain Maxwell, sir, so spare yourself his tears."
Says I, "I'll not but send you shot to buzz about your ears."

Well, they fired as we hove anchor, boys, and we got underway,
But scarce a dozen broadsides, boys, the *Nancy* they did pay
Before the business sickened them. They bravely ran away.
All sail we made, and reached the lake before the close of day.

Aboard the *Nancy*!
We sent them shot and cheers.
Aboard the *Nancy*!
We watched them running through the trees, aboard the *Nancy*-o.

Oh, military gentlemen, they bluster, roar and pray.
Nine sailors and the *Nancy*, boys, made fifty run away.
The powder in their hair that day was powder sent their way
By poor and ragged sailor men, who swore that they would stay.

Aboard the *Nancy*!
Sixpence and found a day
Aboard the *Nancy*!
No uniforms for men to scorn, aboard the *Nancy*-o.

Appendix B

Commodore Sinclair's Report, Also Documents Captured

[DNA, RG 45, CL, 1814, Vol. 6 no. 10 M125, Roll 39]

Captain Arthur Sinclair to The Honorable William Jones, Secretary of the Navy, Washington

US Sloop *Niagara* Erie. Septr. the 3d, 1814
Sir

Immediately after the attack on Michilimackinac, I dispatched the *Lawrence* and *Caledonia* with orders to Lt. Comdt. Dexter to make all possible dispatch to Lake Erie, and there cooperate with our Army &ct, while I shaped my course in pursuit of the Enemies force supposed to be about Nautauwasauga and I cannot but express my surprise at having past those vessels and arrived at Erie before them — By that opportunity I apprised you of my movements up to the 9th Ulto. — since which time I have been fortunate enough to find his BM Schooner *Nancy,* loaded with provision, Clothing &ct for the Troops at Mackinac.

She was two miles up the Nautausasauga River moored under a Block House strongly situated on the S E side of the River, which running nearly parallel with the Bay shore for that distance forms a narrow peninsula — this and the wind being off shore afforded me an opportunity of anchoring opposite to him and within good battering distance; but finding the sand Hills and

Trees frequently interrupting my shot — I borrowed an 8 1/2 inch Howitzer from Colnl Croghan, [Lt. Colonel George Croghan, commander of U.S. military forces on the expedition] mounted it on one of my carriages and sent it on the Peninsula under command of Lieut Holdup — a situation was chosen, by Capt Gratiot of the Engineers, from which it did great execution — The Enemy defended himself very handsomely, until one of those shells burst in his Block House, and in a few minutes blew up his magazine — This set fire to a train which had been laid for the destruction of the vessel, and in an instant she was in flames — had made the necessary preparations with boats for getting aboard her, but frequent and heavy explosions below deck made the risque of lives too great to attempt saving her — she was therefore, with her valuable Cargo, entirely consumed — I cannot say whether those who defended her were blown up in the Block House of whether they retreated in the rear of their work, which they might have done unseen by us, as it afforded a descent into a thick woods — I hope the latter — A number of articles were picked up at a considerable distance off — among them was the Commanders Desk, containing copies of letters &ct; several of which I herewith inclose to you for your information — They serve to shew the vessel to have been commanded by Lieut Worsely [sic] of the Royal Navy, of what infinite importance her cargo was to the garrison at Mackinac, and that they have nothing onfloat now on that Lake — The *Nancy* appeared to be a very fine vessel between the size of the *Queen Charlotte* and *Lady Prevost* — There were three guns on the Blockhouse — 2-24 pdrs & 1-6 pdr — I cannot say what was on the vessel as all her ports were closed — I also got a new Boat, called by them a gunboat but unworthy of the name, being calculated to mount only a 24 pound carronade.

The Nautauwasauga is too narrow and over hung with bushes for a vessel to get up except by warping, which prevented my sending gunboats in, or Colnl Croghan from attempting to turn his rear as we saw a number of Indians sulking and occasionally firing across from the bank, it was in this way the only man we had touched was wounded

You will see by the inclosed letters the short state they are in for provision at Michilimackinac and I am assured from the best authority that this the only line of communication by which can be supplied, that of the Grand River being rendered impassible for any thing heavier than a man can carry on his back by 60 portages; I have therefore left the *Scorpion* and *Tigress* to blockade it closely until the season becomes too boisterous for Boat transportation —

This precaution with an early blockade upon the same place in the spring, will insure the government on easy conquest of Mackinac in May or June, and in my opinion the only means of conquering it without a sacrifice of lives as the importance of the place cannot justify —

Colnl Croghan thought it not advisable to Fortify and garrison Nautauwausaga, as the Enemies communication from York is so short and convenient that any force he could leave there would be cut off in the Winter — It appears that the settlement of Green Bay, on Lake Michigan, can sell from 1 to 3000 bushels of grain which no doubt will be secured by the Enemy during the Winter — Their crops were yet growing when I left that country — should it now meet your approbation I will order a vessel or two up immediately to secure it, and in case of refusal to sell to the U States, as it seems they are favourable to the Enemy, a force of 100 men can destroy it — Any measure respecting it must be immediately taken, as the Navigation in that quarter is unsafe after this month.

I was unfortunate in getting embayed in a gale of wind on a rocky Ironbound shore which occasioned the loss of all the boats I had in tow, among which was the captured gunboat and my Launch — I felt fortunate, however, in saving my vessel, lumbered as she was with 450 souls onboard, and shipping such immense quantities of water as to give me very serious alarm for some hours — I was compelled to strike some of my guns below, and nothing saved her, at least, but a sudden shift of wind, as there is nothing like anchorage in Lake Huron, except in the mouths of Rivers — the whole coast being a steep perpendicular Rock — I have been several times in great danger of total loss, in this extremely dangerous navigation, entirely unknown to our Pilots except direct to Mackinac, by falling suddenly from no soundings into 3 fathoms & twice into ? less twain — all a craggy rock.

Those dangers might be avoided from the transparency of the water; but for the continued thick Fogs with prevail almost as constantly as on the Grand Bank —By the arrival of the mail a few hours after I anchored at Detroit, I learned the critical state of our army on the Peninsula, and that the *Somers* and *Ohio* had been captured — The Craft from the Flats, with part of my Guns and shot had not yet arrived; but being certain my presence would be necessary at the earliest possible moment I availed myself of a fair wind and sailed for this place — where I am happy to learn that our Army feel themselves perfectly secure where they are — I have hence sent the *Lawrence, Lady Prevost* and *Porcupine* to

Buffalo, there to render any assistance which may be required, and shall follow them myself in the course of 24 Hours — There is such an eminent risqué of the loss of the Fleet at this season of the year — laying to an anchor near Buffalo, where the Bottom is composed entirely of sharp Rock, a strong current setting down, and exposed to the open lake from whence the heaviest gales are experienced, that I shall not, unless ordered positively to do so from the Department, continue there a moment longer than I can ascertain the commanding officer's views and in what way the Fleet can cooperate with him — Daily and dear bought experience teaches us we ought not to risqué our Fleet in a situation, where they are so liable to be lost — Lieut Kennedy has, no doubt, informed you of the Total loss of the *Ariel* after being afloat and ready to move from there — a large number of my best men's times are out and no argument or policy I can see can prevail on them to remain, even to go down to Buffalo and I cannot use force as they have served already several months of their time — I shall stop the outfits of the *Queen Charlotte* immediately on my return here, unless I find she may be absolutely necessary as a Transport for some movement the Army may have in contemplation, as I have not a sufficiency of men nor to man well more than 12 of the guns onboard either the *Lawrence* or this vessel — I have not had time to look round me sufficiently since my arrival, to give you the state of things here — Lieut Kennedy, however, informs me that the lighters were too much decayed to get the *Detroit* over the Bar, which will induce me to leave the *Caledonia* here to protect her from surprise until I can have Lighters built, which I have ordered to be immediately done — The *Caledonia* is unseaworthy, from natural decay — I would recommend her, the *Amelia* and perhaps the *Hunter* to be sold, being all nearly in the same state —

I have the Honor to remain with great respect, Sir, your Obt Servt

A Sinclair
[Commander of U.S. Lake Erie squadron]

N.B. — A company of Riflemen from Sandusky has just arrived here & have been forwarded on to Fort Erie without delay —

[Enclosure 1]

Michilimackinac 28th July 1814

Sir

The American Expedition destined for the attack of this Island, having at length made its appearance, under the Command of Commodore Elliott [sic] and Lt. Colonel Croghan, consisting of the *Niagara* 20 Guns, *Lawrence* 20 Guns, *Hunter* Brig 8 Guns, a Large Schooner of — Guns, the *Mary* of — Guns, five Gun boats and the *Mink*, their prize, I hasten to apprise you of this Circumstance lest the *Nancy* and valuable Cargo, fall into their hands, and that you may be enabled to take such steps for their preservation as will appear to you most expedient under the present Circumstances — I have taken such precautions as were in my power, to make you acquainted with this Event in case you should be upon you passage — If so, I would recommend you to return to the Nottawasaga River, and to take the *Nancy* as high as possible — place her in a judicious position, and hastily run up a strong log house, such as were made when the boats were built but larger with Loop Holes and Embrasures for your two six pounders which will enable you to defend her should you be attacked which not unlikely —

The mode of obtaining her Cargo of such value to us, will depend upon the result of the attack which we daily expect and on the duration of the Blockade, I see no other way of obtaining the Provisions but by bringing them in Batteaux, protected by the Carronades in the Bows of two of them

I have the Honor to be Sir Your most obt Servt

(signed) Rt McDowall Lt. Col
Commanding at Michilimackinac
[Lt. Col. Robert McDouall, British commanding officer at Michilimackinac]

You will probably receive instructions from Kingston as to your Conduct —

[Enclosure 2]

Extract from a letter to W D Thomas Esqr. M.D. Surgeon, 104 Regt. York or Kingston —

dated Nautawasauga River 6th Aug 1814

It is now nearly a month since I left York in company with Lieut. Worsley of the Navy on my way to the Land of promise, but things have turned out rather unfortunately, for you still behold me a sojourner in this wilderness. We had waited about a week on the Banks of this River before the *Nancy* arrived, during which time we suffered every misery that you can imagine from bad weather and meriads of musquettos &c &c — The land here is the most barren I have seen and seems to have been formed from time to time by the washing of Lake Huron, it being for upwards of two miles composed entirely of banks of sand, on which nothing grows but small brush wood. We found a number of Indians encamped on the Lake shore who were extremely troublesome before the vessel arrived, and it was not possible to keep them out of our Wigwams. You may therefore judge what a pleasant sight the *Nancy* was for us, we found her a very fine schooner with an admirable cabin, her cargo was not completed before Sunday last, and she got under way on Monday with every prospect of reaching Mackinac in a short time which is only 220 miles from hence. We had been out but for a few hours, when we met an express from Col. McDouall to say that the American Squadron from Lake Erie of large forces was Blockading the Island, and that we could not possibly reach it, we therefore had the mortification to put back into this wretched place where we are busily employed in erecting a Block House to contain and defend the Stores and Schooner in case of an attack which is an event I have no doubt of; but I hope from the strength of the fine ground Worsley has chosen, and the good of his crew, that we shall be able to beat off a very strong force — The River is too narrow to sail up, we shall therefore only have Gun boats to contend with — I hope Mackinac Provisions for 3 months, and the Enemy it is said cannot keep out so long on account of the climate, so that the *Nancy* can make a run late in the season with the Stores, if we succeed in defending them — I expect the man [Robert Livingston] who brought the express the other day, who has gone to York, and intends going back to Mackinac in a canoe — I shall trust my person to him, as he thinks he can again give Jonathan the Slip.

[Assistant Surgeon Thomas Sampson? Royal Newfoundland Regiment]

[Enclosure 3]

By Commodore Sir James
Lucas Yeo Kt., Commanding his
Majesty's Ships and Vessels
Employed on the Lakes in
Canada &c &c &c

You are hereby required and directed to proceed to Lake Huron, and take upon yourself the Charge and Command of the Naval Establishment on that Lake —

In the execution of this Service you are strictly enjoined to cooperate most cordially with Lieut Colonel McDowell, the Military officer Commanding the Forces in that Quarter —

You are to be particular that a proper course of discipline and good order is observed in the parts placed under your command — and to transmit to me by every opportunity the particulars of the Service you are employed on; also to keep a Journal of your Proceedings, which is to be transmitted to me every Six Months —

Given under my hand on Board his Majesty's Ship *Wolfe,* at Kingston in Upper Canada, this tenth day of February 1814 —

(Signed) James Lucas Yeo
[Commander of British naval forces on the Great Lakes]

To Lieut. Newdegate Poyntz

Appointed to command the Naval Establishment
on Lake Huron

[Lieutenant Newdegate Poyntz, Royal Navy, was subsequently superceded by Lt. Worsley]

[Enclosure 4]

Dear Sir,

The bearer, Lt. Worsley, is appointed to supercede Mr. Poyntz in the Command of your Flotilla, & I beg to introduce Him to you as an excellent naval officer & fine honorable young man.

    Col. Tucker is come out to the 41st & with that Regt. some Militia & Military will proceed to Erie to watch the motions of the enemy's force there. —

Wishing you every success for there is no chance of Peace, I am yrs. very truly

W Howe Mulcaster
[Commander William Howe Mulcaster, Royal Navy stationed on Lake Ontario]

I got hit in the thigh at Oswego but am getting better —
Kingston U.C. June 25th 1814

Appendix C

McDouall's Report on Worsley's War

[Library and Archives Canada/British and Naval Records fonds/RG 8, vol. 685 pg. 176-178]

Michilmackinac 9 September 1814

Sir,

I have the honor to inform you that some Indians, on their way to the falls of St. Mary's, returned to me with the intelligence, that part of the enemy's Squadron had on the 25th ulto: again made their appearance in the neighbourhood of St. Joseph's likewise occupying the passage of the Detour, their intention being evidently to cut of supplies, & prevent all communication with this Garrison.

On the 31st I was joined by Lieut: Worsley of the Royal Navy with seventeen seamen, who had passed in a canoe sufficiently near the Enemy to ascertain them to be two schooner rigged Gun Boats of the largest class. On stating to me his opinion that they might be attacked with every prospect of success, particularly as they were at anchor nearly five leagues asunder, I immediately determined to furnish him with requisite assistance.

In the course of the next day, four Boats were accordingly equipped, two of them with field pieces in their bows, One of them was manned by the seamen of the navy, the remaining three by a detachment of the Royal Newfoundland Reg't under Lieut Bulger, Armstrong and Radenhurst, consisting of fifty men. The whole sailed the same evening under the command of Lieut Worsley.

I have now the satisfaction of reporting to you the complete success of the expedition. Lieut Worsley having returned to this place, on the 7th inst. With his two prizes, consisting of the U.S. schooners *Scorpion* and *Tigress*, the former carrying a long 24 and a long 12 pr, and the latter a long 24, they were commanded by Lieut: Turner of the American Navy, and are very fine vessels. For the particulars of their Capture, I beg leave to refer you to the inclosed statement of Lieut Bulger, whose conduct in aiding the Execution of this enterprise (in which he was slightly wounded) reflects upon his great credit, & I beg leave to recommend him as a meritorioius officer of long standing, who has been in many of the actions of this War. Lieut Armstrong & Radenhurst possess similar claims, & whith the detachment of the brave Newfoundland Regiment (who are familiar with this kind of service) merit my entire approbation, neither should I omit noticing the zeal displayed by Mr. Dickson and Lieut Livingston of the Indian department, who volunteered their services on this occasion.—

In calling your attention to the conspicuousment of the officer who so judiciously planed & carried into effect this well concerted enterprise — I am conscious that I only do Lieut Worsely a strict justice in acknowledging the eminent services which he has rendered this Garrison — You are already acquainted with the inequal conflict which he sustained at the Mouth of the River Nottawasaga and the almost unprecedented defence which he made of the *Nancy* schooner with only twenty one seamen and a few Indians, against the American squadron & upwards of three hundred troops. Since that period he with his gallant little band of seamen, has traversed the extensive Lake in two boats laden with provisions for the garrison, & having at this extremity of it, discovered two of his former opponents, his active and indefatigable mind rested not, till he had relieved us from such troublesome neighbours and conducted the blockading force in triumph into our Post.

Such Sir, have been the services of Lt Worsley during the short time that he ahs been stationed on Lake Huron. I have to beg that you will strongly recommend him to the protection of Commodore Sir James Yeo & also to the patronage of His Excellency the Governor General in order that my Lords Commissioners of the Admiralty may be enabled to appreciate them as they merit.

I have the honor to be

Sir Your most obedt Servant

Rt. McDouall
Lt. Col. Comg at Michilimackinac
[Lt. Col. Robert McDouall, British commanding officer at Michilimackinac]

Addressed to Lieut Genl. Drummond
[Lt. General Gordon Drummond, commander of British military forces in Upper Canada]

Appendix D

Robert Livingston's War Record

[Library and Archives Canada/British and Naval Records fonds/RG 8, vol. 258 pg. 118 — 124c]

To His Excellency Sir Gordon Drummond, Knight Commander of the Most Honorable and Military Order of the Bath, Administrator in Chief of the Government of the Provinces of Upper and lower Canada, Vice Admiral of the same, &c., &c., &c.

The petition of Robert Livingston, late captain in the Indian Department, Respectfully sheweth

That your Petitioner at the beginning of the late American war was living in a very comfortable way at the Island of St. Joseph's, through always anxious to do anything that might come within the Sphere of his Power to promote the Interest and welfare of Government. That he accepted the Situation of Adjutant and Quartermaster of the volunteer militia, which were then raising the St. Joseph's for the purpose of making a descent on the Enemie's Post of Michilimackinac, thirty-six of which men your Petitioner procured himself, & which situation he conceived himself quite adequate to fulfill, having formerly served nine & half years in the second Battalion of the late Royal Canadian Volunteers.

That your Petitioner, after the capture of Michilimackinac, was ordered by Captain Roberts of the 10th Royal Vn Battalion, who commanded, to proceed to Detroit, with the Prisoners of War, which service he duly performed and saved their lives from the Indians, who were lying in Ambush, as they were descending the River Saint Clair. —

That on his arrival at Detroit he was made Prisoner of War, from whence he made his escape the third night and arrived at Amherstburg, where he put himself under the Command of Lieutenant Colonel St. George, who commanded that Garrison, two days after he was wounded and taken prisoner at the battle of Brownstown, and was again carried into the Garrison of Detroit, at which place he remained a Prisoner until the Capture of that Garrison by the British Forces under the Command of the late General Brock on the sixteenth day of August, one thousand eight hundred and twelve. Immediately after the Capture of which place he was ordered by General Brock to proceed to Michilimackinac, with Public Dispatches, at which place he arrived on the twenty fourth day of August from thence he was ordered to proceed to Saint Joseph's, there to perform the duties of an interpreter until further orders, in the month of January ensuing he was ordered by Captain Roberts to repair to Michilimackinac, from thence was ordered to Detroit with Public Dispatches, at which place he arrived on the twelfth day of February, one thousand eight hundred and thirteen. That he remained at Detroit, nineteen days and was again ordered to Michilimackinac with Dispatches, at which place he arrived on the twelfth day of March, he remained there but four days, when he was again ordered to St. Joseph's, making in all a distance of six hundred and sixty miles or thereabouts, which was performed on snowshoes, and sleeping out the whole time in a single blanket and starving for want of provisions. —

That your Petitioner was in the month of July, one thousand eight hundred and thirteen, ordered to proceed to and join the army under the command of General De Rottenburg, then quartered on the Four Mile Creek, (Niagara Frontier,) to pass by the North Side of Lake Huron and raise and take with him the Indians residing in that Quarter, which Service he punctually performed and arrived at the Headquarters of the Army commanded by General De Rottenburg, on the ninth day of August, from which time to the seventeenth of the same month he kept the Indians, who came with him, in constant motion by every day annoying the Enemy's Picquets, and frequently brought in Prisoners and Scalps. On the Seventeenth he received four severe wounds and was again taken prisoner. By those wounds he is in a great measure deprived of the Sight of his right eye by the blow of a Tomahawk, which he received from the Inimical Indians. Is also deprived of the Natural use of his right arm owing to the Stab of a Spear which he received in his Shoulder, and was also wounded in the head, the fourth wound is a musket-ball in his left thigh, which remains unextracted.

That your Petitioner was in this situation carried into the Fort of Old Niagara where he was treated with the greatest inhumanity, being refused the least medical aid until his wounds were swarming with worms. That on the Night of the nineteenth of October, (notwithstanding he was very ill of his wounds) he effected his escape, subsisting seven days on acorns alone. On the first day of November he reached Burlington Heights and again joined the advance at Stoney Creek under the command of Lieutenant Colonel Murray. That he remained with the advance until after the Capture of all the enemies posts on the Niagara Frontier, altho' at the same time not well of his former wounds, two of which remain still open. Shortly after the Capture of those Posts he was ordered to proceed to Michilimackinac, with an Escort of Indians with Public Money, which voyage he performed and returned to Fort George on the twenty eighth day of March one thousand eight hundred and fourteen, where he remained but four days when he was again ordered to proceed to Nottowassogay, there to join the Detachment of the Newfoundland Regiment under the Command of Lieutenant Colonel McDouall, to act as guide and conductor to them on their Route to Michilimackinac, which service was duly performed. And if that Detachment arrived Safe it was owing to the vigilance of their conductor. Immediately after his arrival at Michilimackinac a guide was wanted to conduct the schooner *Nancy* to the River Nottowassaugay. As no other person could be found capable of undertaking this hazardous piece of Service, and the Safety of the garrison much depended on the Success of this voyage, your petitioner without hesitation embarked, and guided the vessel to the River Nottawassaugay, two hundred and fifty miles along a very dangerous and unexplored Coast, and in nine days returned to Michilimackinac with the vessel, Crew and cargo, all safe. No other person in that Country could be found who was capable of undertaking this service. That shortly after the Enemies fleet made its appearance off Michilimackinac, at which time he was ordered to proceed in a canoe through their Fleet to go in pursuit of the schooner *Nancy*, which was then on her way from Nottowasaugay to Michilimackinac in order that her Commander might take the necessary precaution to keep her from falling into the hands of the Enemy, which Service Your Petitioner performed, and actually met the *Nancy* on her way to

Michilimackinac, but according to Lieut. Col. McDouall's instructions, turned her Back to the River Nattaawassaugay. That he proceeded, according to his Instructions, to York with Dispatches and returned with all possible expedition anxious to afford the *Nancy*'s commander all the assistance in his Power.

That your Petitioner rejoined her crew on the twelfth day of August just as the Enemy's Squadron made its appearance off the Harbour of Nottawassaugay. That he immediately collected all the Indians in that vicinity, being in number but twenty-three, and gave what assistance was in his Power to Lieutenant Worsley, having after a gallant and very vigorous defence of one whole day's Duration, with twenty-one Indians, nine Canadians and twenty seamen, combated with three hundred and Eighty of the Enemy.

And your Petitioner does on this Occasion claim the Credit of Saving that brave officer and his Gallant little Crew from falling into the hands of the Enemy; afterwards he conducted Lieutenant Worsley and Crew to Michilimackinac, in two Batteaux and one Canoe, loaded with Provisions; passed three hundred and sixty miles of the North Side of Lake Huron which voyage was performed in seven days and a half, that on their way they fell in with two of the Enemies Schooners, which were Blockading the Detour (a narrow passage which they were obliged to pass) they secured all the Provisions in the two Batteaux and secured them in an Obscure Bay. That they took all the men into his Canoe, being in number thirty-five, passed the Blockading Squadron at the distance of one hundred yards in the night and arrived Safe at Michilimackinac on the first day of September, when immediate application was made for assistance by Lieutenant Worsley, which assistance was granted, and that our Petitioner and Lieutenant Worsley returned, boarded & took the two schooners, the first on the fifth and the second on the seventh day of September, and the appeals to Lieutenant Worsley (who commanded this expedition) and the other officers under his command, to know if his services on this occasion were not of the utmost importance, in quality of Pilot he will venture to say not another person could be found in all that Country who was capable of performing this Important Service.

That your petitioner was, immediately after his capture, ordered with a guard of Indians to conduct the officers and seamen taken on board the two vessels to York, which service he performed and returned to Michilimackinac on the twelfth day of October, where he obtained permission to go to Montreal to pass the Winter in the month of January, one thousand eight hundred and fifteen, when your Petitioner was appointed Captain of the Indian Department he was again ordered to proceed to Michilimackinac with Lieutenant Colonel McKay, at which place he arrived on the twelfth day of March after a very fatiguing journey, three hundred and sixty miles of which were on Show Shoes.

That your Petitioner has travelled as bearer of Public Dispatches and by orders of the different officers under whose command he has been since the commencement of the late war eight thousand eight hundred and ninety miles, for which he has never received any traveling expenses, allowances or anything in lieu thereof. Your Petitioner lost his Establishment at St. Joseph's, viz. House, Wharf and Store, which were burn't by the Enemy, and has lost his health, Strength & Comfort for the good of his country, a country which never allows her brave sons to go unprotected or unrewarded and upon which Country and the Justice of Your Honor our Petitioner reposes with confidence —

That your Honor may be convinced of the truth of your Petitioner's Representation and of his just expectation of Protection from this generous government he has subjoined a certificate of the deserving and worthy men (who are generally known to your Excellency) as to your Petitioners Service and his claims on the Country he has so served.

That by a Garrison order at Michilimackinac, dated the tenth day of July last, several officers of the Indian Department were reduced and the case of Your Petitioner reserved for consideration of Your Excellency, therefore, with the greatest confidence and most lively hope your petitioner submits his case to the Consideration and Justice of Your Excellency, and

Humbly Prays that Your Excellency will be pleased to grant him that justice and relief that his Case in the opinion of Your Excellency may merit, And as in duty bound your Petitioner shall ever pray.

Robert Livingston
12 July 1815

Notes

CHAPTER 1: THE OLD NORTHWEST

1   Ontario, Ministry of Natural Resources, *HMS Nancy and the War of 1812*. Toronto: Government of Ontario Publications, 1978.

2   C.H.J. Snider, *Leaves from the War Log of the Nancy* (Midland, Ont.: Huronia Historical Development Council, 1936), ix. The family name is sometimes spelled McIntosh when referring to both Angus and his sons. For clarity, the Mackintosh spelling has been adopted throughout this work.

3   Ronald Hoskins, "Angus Mackintosh, the Baron of Moy Hall," in *The Western District: Papers from the Western District Conference*, ed. K.G. Pryke and L.L. Kulisek (Windsor, Ont.: Essex County Historical Society, 1983), 147.

4   In one particular instance, the *Caledonia* took fur packs for the Michigan and South West Fur Company to Fort Erie. John Askin Jr. to John Askin Sr., 16 September 1812, in *The John Askin Papers*, ed. Milo M. Quaife (Detroit: Detroit Library Commission, 1928), 2:733.

5   John Askin Sr. to John Askin Jr., 31 July 1810, *Askin Papers*, 2:658.

6   Ernest A. Cruikshank, "An Episode of the War of 1812: The Story of the Schooner *Nancy*," in *The Defended Border*, ed. Morris Zaslow (Toronto: Macmillan, 1964), 143.

7   *HMS Nancy and the War of 1812.*

8   Ernest J. Lajeunesse, ed., *The Windsor Border Region: Canada's Southernmost Frontier, A Collection of Documents* (Toronto: Champlain Society, 1960), xli–li.

9   Max Rosenberg, *The Building of Perry's Fleet on Lake Erie, 1812–1813* (Harrisburg, Pa.: Pennsylvania Historical and Museum Commission, 1997), 12–13.

10 Hunter to the Duke of Kent, 1800, in *Michigan Pioneer and Historical Society Collection* (Lansing, Mich.: Robert Smith Printing Company, 1889), 15:8–24.

11 Rosenberg, *The Building of Perry's Fleet*, 15.

12 Alec R. Gilpin, *The War of 1812 in the Old Northwest* (East Lansing, Mich.: Michigan State University Press, 1958), 31.

13 William Gray, *Soldiers of the King: The Upper Canada Militia 1812–1815, A Reference Guide* (Erin, Ont.: Boston Mills Press, 1995), 18.

14 For a full discussion, see G. Terry Sharrer, "The Search for a Naval Policy, 1783–1812," in Kenneth J. Hagan ed., *In Peace and War: Interpretations of American Naval History, 1775-1984* (Westport, Conn.: Greenwood, 1984), 33–40.

15 Reginald Horsman, *The War of 1812* (New York: Alfred A. Knopf, 1969), 11–16.

16 See, for example, Horsman, *The War of 1812*, 15–16; Gilpin, *The War of 1812 in the Old Northwest*, 40; Sandy Antal, *A Wampum Denied: Procter's War of 1812* (Ottawa: Carleton University Press, 1997), 14–18. Most writers on the western War of 1812 stress the importance of western issues in driving the United States' declaration of war.

17 Cruikshank, "An Episode of the War of 1812," 144.

18 J. Mackay Hitsman, *The Incredible War of 1812: A Military History* (Toronto: Robin Brass, 1999), 8.

19 A.H. Pye, Report on the Provincial Marine of the Canadas, 7 December 1811, in *Select British Documents of the Canadian War of 1812*, ed. William Wood (Toronto: Champlain Society, 1923), 1:241.

20 Pye, Report on the Provincial Marine, 1:242.

21 Gray to Prevost, 24 February 1812, *Select British Documents of the Canadian War of 1812*, 1:253–54; Pye, Report on the Provincial Marine, 1:242.

22 Gray to Prevost, 24 February 1812, *Select British Documents of the Canadian War of 1812*, 1:254. Emphasis in original.

23 David Curtis Skaggs and Gerard T. Altoff, *A Signal Victory: The Lake Erie Campaign 1812–1813* (Annapolis, Md.: Naval Institute Press, 1997), 25.

24 Robert Malcomson, *Lords of the Lake: The Naval War on Lake Ontario, 1812–1814* (Toronto: Robin Bass Studio, 1998), 20; Woolsey to Hamilton, 26 June 1812, *The Naval War of 1812: A Documentary History*, ed. William S. Dudley and Michael Crawford (Washington: Navy Historical Center, 1985), 1:277–78.

25 Gray, Memoranda on the Defensive Strength and Equipment of the North West Company, *Select British Documents of the Canadian War of 1812*, 1:286.

26 Cruikshank, "An Episode of the War of 1812," 144.

27 Gray to Prevost, 13 January 1812, *Select British Documents of the Canadian War of 1812*, 1:283–85. Emphasis in original.

28 Hitsman, *The Incredible War of 1812*, 25.

29 Wesley B. Turner, *British Generals in the War of 1812: High Command in the Canadas* (Montreal: McGill-Queen's University Press, 1999), 25–26.

30 Hitsman, *The Incredible War of 1812*, 31.

31 For a sympathetic description of Prevost's strategic situation, see Hitsman, *The Incredible War of 1812*, 41–44.

32 Gray to Prevost, 13 January 1812, *Select British Documents of the Canadian War of 1812*, 1:284.

33 Minutes of Company annual meeting, 18 July 1812, in W. Stewart Wallace, ed., *Documents Relating to the North West Company* (Toronto: Champlain Society, 1934), 271.

34 Brock to Prevost, 2 December 1811, *Select British Documents of the Canadian War of 1812*, 1:271.

35 *Ibid.*, 1:275.

36 Skaggs and Altoff, *A Signal Victory*, 23.

37 John A. Garraty and Mark C. Carnes, eds., *Dictionary of American National Biography* (New York: Oxford University Press, 1999), 11:455–56; and Donald R. Hickey, *The War of 1812: A Forgotten Conflict* (Urbana, Ill.: University of Illinois Press, 1989), 80–81.

38 St. George to Brock, 8 July 1812, *Michigan Pioneer and Historical Society Collection*, 15:97–98.

39 *Ibid.*, 15:103–104.

40 Proclamation of Hull, 13 July 1812, *Select British Documents of the Canadian War of 1812*, 1:357.

41 Brock to Prevost, 20 July 1812, in Ernest Cruikshank, ed., *The Documentary History of the Campaign on the Niagara Frontier* (Welland, Ont.: Lundy's Lane Historical Society, 1908), 3:133.

42 Antal, *A Wampum Denied*, 52.

43 *Buffalo Gazette*, 4 August 1814, in *The Documentary History of the Campaign on the Niagara Frontier*, 3:165.

44 Skaggs and Altoff, *A Signal Victory*, 23.

45 Gilpin, *The War of 1812 in the Old Northwest*, 90; Barry Gough, *Fighting Sail on Lake Huron and Georgian Bay: The War of 1812 and its Aftermath* (Annapolis, Md.: Naval Institute Press, 2002), 16–18.

46 Hanks to Hull, 4 August 1812, in Ernest Cruikshank, ed., *Documents Relating to the Invasion of Canada and the Surrender of Detroit* (Ottawa: Government Printing Bureau, 1912), 67.

47 Roberts to Brock, 17 July 1812, *Michigan Pioneer and Historical Society Collection*, 15:108.

48 Hanks to Hull, 4 August 1812, *Documents Relating to the Invasion of Canada and the Surrender of Detroit*, 68.

49 Roberts to Brock, 17 July 1812, *Michigan Pioneer and Historical Society Collection*, 15:108.

50 Monthly return of the Garrison at Michilimackinac, June 1812, *ibid.*, 15:115.

51 Gilpin, *The War of 1812 in the Old Northwest*, 90.

52 Hanks to Hull, 4 August 1812, *Documents Relating to the Invasion of Canada and the Surrender of Detroit*, 68.

53 Capitulation of Michilimackinac, 17 July 1812, *Michigan Pioneer and Historical Society Collection*, 15:110.

54 Askin to unknown, 18 July 1812, *ibid.*, 15:113.

55 See, for example, Hitsman, *The Incredible War of 1812*, 75; and George F.G. Stanley, *The War of 1812: Land Operations* (Toronto: Macmillan, 1983), 112.

56 Charles Askin, diary, 16 August 1812, *Documents Relating to the Invasion of Canada and the Surrender of Detroit*, 241.

57 Skaggs and Altoff, *A Signal Victory*, 34.

58 Antal, *A Wampum Denied*, 67.

59 *Dictionary of Canadian Biography*, 6:616–17.

60 Charles Askin, diary, 17 August 1812, *Documents Relating to the Invasion of Canada and the Surrender of Detroit*, 242.

61 General Return of Prisoners of War, 16 August 1812. The table accounts for 2,188 prisoners, including those captured at Michilimackinac. National Archives of Canada, RG 8 I 688B — 6.

62 Charles Askin, diary, 18 August 1812, *Documents Relating to the Invasion of Canada and the Surrender of Detroit*, 243.

63 Brock to Prevost, 11 October 1812, *The Naval War of 1812: A Documentary History*, 1:332.

CHAPTER 2: A SHIPBUILDER'S WAR

64 Skaggs and Altoff, *A Signal Victory*, 34.

65 Hamilton to Chauncey, 31 August 1812, *The Naval War of 1812: A Documentary History*, 1:297.

66 Rosenberg, *The Building of Perry's Fleet*, 7–8 and 22.

67 *Ibid.*, 23.

68 Memorial to His Excellency Sir George Prevost, Baronet, Captain General and Governor in the Chief in and over the Provinces of Lower Canada, Upper Canada, &c &c &c., *Michigan Pioneer and Historical Society Collection*, 15:252.

69 Antal, *A Wampum Denied*, 209.

70 Robert S. Quimby, *The U.S. Army in the War of 1812: An Operational and Command Study* (2 vols.; East Lansing, Mich.: Michigan State University Press, 1997), 1:92.

71 See Quimby, *The U.S. Army in the War of 1812*, 1:109; Hickey, *Forgotten Conflict*, 85; and Gilpin, *The War of 1812 in the Old Northwest*, 155–58.

72 Antal, *A Wampum Denied*, 167.

73 *Ibid.*, 167; and Gilpin, *The War of 1812 in the Old Northwest*, 167.

74 Gilpin, *The War of 1812 in the Old Northwest*, 167–68.

75 Antal, *A Wampum Denied*, 171–72.

76   Troop Return for the Battle of the River Raisin, RG 8 I C 695-51.

77   Quimby, *The U.S. Army in the War of 1812*, 1:136.

78   Richard Barbuto, *Niagara, 1814: America Invades Canada* (Lawrence, Kans.: University Press of Kansas, 2000), 94; and Gilpin, *The War of 1812 in the Old Northwest*, 170.

79   Quimby, *The U.S. Army in the War of 1812*, 1:139–40.

80   Chauncey to Jones, 18 March 1813, *The Naval War of 1812: A Documentary History*, 2:430–432.

81   Donald Hickey views Kingston as the primary American target (*The War of 1812: A Forgotten Conflict*, 127–29). While this was Armstrong's original plan, Chauncey and Dearborn proposed an alternate one, which was carried out in the spring of 1813. See Quimby, *The U.S. Army in the War of 1812*, 1:222–24; Horsman, *The War of 1812*, 91; and J.C.A. Stagg, *Mr. Madison's War: Politics, Diplomacy and Warfare in the Early American Republic, 1783–1830* (Princeton, N.J.: Princeton University Press, 1983), 286.

82   Embarkation Return of the Western Army Commanded by Brigadier General Procter on an Expedition to the Miamis, 23 April 1813, *Select British Documents of the Canadian War of 1812*, 2:38.

83   Gilpin, *The War of 1812 in the Old Northwest*, 175; Antal, *A Wampum Denied*, 218–19; Harrison to Armstrong, 5 May 1813, in Logan Esarey, ed., *Messages and Letters of William Henry Harrison* (New York: Arno Press, 1975), 2:432.

84   Alexander Clark Casselman, in *Richardson's War of 1812, with Notes and a Life of the Author by Alexander Clark Casselman* (Toronto: Coles, 1974), 148.

85   Casselman, *Richardson's War*, 148–49; Harrison to Armstrong, 13 May 1813, *Messages and Letters of William Henry Harrison*, 2:445.

86   Procter to Prevost, 14 May 1813, *Select British Documents of the Canadian War of 1812*, 2:34.

87   Casselman, *Richardson's War*, 160–61.

88   Statement of Militia Captains, 6 May, *Michigan Pioneer and Historical Society Collection*, 15:280.

89   Procter to Prevost, 14 May 1813, *Select British Documents of the Canadian War of 1812*, 2:35.

90   Dearborn to Armstrong, 28 April 1813, *The Naval War of 1812: A Documentary History*, 2:451.

91   Sheaffe to Prevost, 5 May 1813, *ibid.*, 2:455–56.

92   Carl Benn, *The Battle of York* (Belleville, Ont.: Mika Publishing, 1984), 38.

93   *Ibid.*, 39; and Dearborn to Armstrong, 28 April 1813, *The Naval War of 1812: A Documentary History*, 2:451.

94   Benn, *The Battle of York*, 51.

95   Perry to Jones, 19 June 1813, *The Naval War of 1812: A Documentary History*, 2:481.

96   John Marshall, *Royal Naval Biography* (London: Longman, Reese, Orme, Brown and Green, 1831), 186–87.

97   Procter to McDouall, 4 July 1813, *Select British Documents of the Canadian War of 1812*, 2:40–41.

98   *Ibid.*, 2:43.

99   Procter to McDonall, 29 June 1813, *Michigan Pioneer and Historical Society Collection*, 15:325–26.

100   Procter to Prevost, 9 August 1813, *Select British Documents of the Canadian War of 1812*, 2:44.

101   Harrison to Armstrong, 23 July 1813, *Messages and Letters of William Henry Harrison*, 2:494.

102   Clay to Harrison, 26 July 1813, *Messages and Letters of William Henry Harrison*, 2:499.

103   Casselman, *Richardson's War*, 177–78.

104   Clay to Harrison, 26 July 1813, *Messages and Letters of William Henry Harrison*, 2:499.

105   Snider, *Leaves from the War Log of the Nancy*, vii.

106   Gilpin, *The War of 1812 in the Old Northwest*, 202.

107   Snider, *Leaves from the War Log of the Nancy*, vii.

108   Procter to Prevost, 9 August 1813, *Select British Documents of the Canadian War of 1812*, 2:44.

109   Snider, *Leaves from the War Log of the Nancy*, viii.

110   *Ibid.*, xi.

111   *Ibid.*

112 *Ibid.*, xii.

113 Procter to Prevost, 9 August 1813, *Select British Documents of the Canadian War of 1812*, 2:45.

114 Horsman, *The War of 1812*, 102–103; Gilpin, *The War of 1812 in the Old Northwest*, 206–207.

115 Procter to Prevost, 9 August 1813, *Select British Documents of the Canadian War of 1812*, 2:45-46. Procter's movements in the spring of 1813 are also described in Frederick Coyne Hamil, *Michigan in the War of 1812* (Lansing, Mich.: Michigan Historical Commission, 1977), 30.

116 Snider, *Leaves from the War Log of the Nancy*, xiii.

117 Benson John Lossing, *The Pictorial Field-Book of the War of 1812* (New York: Harper, 1868), 512.

118 Rosenberg, *The Building of Perry's Fleet*, 42–43.

119 Cruikshank, "The Contest for the Command of Lake Erie," 98.

CHAPTER 3: ABOARD THE NANCY

120 A.T. Mahan, *Sea Power in its Relations to the War of 1812* (Boston: Little, Brown, 1905), 2:74.

121 Prevost to Procter, 22 August 1813, *Select British Documents of the Canadian War of 1812*, 2:49.

122 See, for example, Mahan, *Sea Power*, 2:77; Casselman, *Richardson's War*, 190.

123 G.W.L. Nicholson, *The Fighting Newfoundlander* (n.p.: Government of Newfoundland, 1964), 78–79.

124 Skaggs and Altoff, *A Signal Victory*, 113.

125 See, for example, Mahan, *Sea Power*, 2:81; Cruickshank, "The Contest for the Command of Lake Erie," 98.

126 Skaggs and Altoff, *A Signal Victory*, 135.

127 For further details on the battle of Lake Erie, see Skaggs and Altoff, *A Signal Victory*, 118–48; Mahan, *Sea Power*, 2:93; and Theodore Roosevelt, *The Naval War of 1812, or the History of the United States Navy during the Last War with Great Britain to Which is Appended an Account of the Battle of New Orleans.* (1907; reprinted, Annapolis,

Md.: Naval Institute Press, 1987), 265.

128 Certificate to Richard Pattinson, 22 November 1813, *Michigan Pioneer and Historical Society Collection*, 15:446.

129 Snider, *Leaves from the War Log of the Nancy*, xvi.

130 *Ibid.*, xvi.

131 *Ibid.*, xiv.

132 McIntosh to Bullock, 16 October 1813, *Michigan Pioneer and Historical Society Collection*, 15:412.

133 Snider, *Leaves from the War Log of the Nancy*, xix.

134 Hitsman, *The Incredible War of 1812*, 175–76.

135 Snider, *Leaves from the War Log of the Nancy*, xix.

136 *Ibid.*, vii.

137 *Ibid.*, xix.

138 *Ibid.*

139 McIntosh to Bullock, 16 October 1813, *Michigan Pioneer and Historical Society Collection*, 15:412. Mackintosh only identifies Beaubien as a Canadian, which at the time could have simply meant the man was French-speaking. He gives no clues as to the nationality of the militia that Beaubien commanded. There is no Beaubien listed as an officer in the Essex militia; therefore it would seem that he commanded either a group of disaffected men from Upper Canada or a group of American militia.

140 Snider, *Leaves from the War Log of the Nancy*, xxi.

141 *Ibid.*, xxiii.

142 *Ibid.*, xxviii.

143 *Ibid.*, xxix.

144 McIntosh to Bullock, 16 October 1813, *Michigan Pioneer and Historical Society Collection*, 15:412–13.

145 Snider, *Leaves from the War Log of the Nancy*, xxxiv.

146 Gilpin, *The War of 1812 in the Old Northwest*, 228.

147 Harrison to Secretary of War, 16 October 1813, *The Documentary History of the Campaign on the Niagara Frontier*, 8:71–72.

148 Report by William McKay to Prevost, n.d., *Michigan Pioneer and Historical Society Collection*, 15:656–58. The editors of the collection placed this with documents from 1814, inferring that the canoe-loads of supplies were from a similar expedition in

the fall of 1814. Careful reading of the document, however, suggests that it is actually from the fall of 1813.

149 Report of the Examining Committee, 28 October 1813, cited in Snider, *Leaves from the War Log of the Nancy*, xxxvi.

150 Bullock to Freer, 30 December 1813, *Michigan Pioneer and Historical Society Collection*, 15:465–66.

151 Hitsman, *The Incredible War of 1812*, 216.

152 Sinclair to Cooke, 25 August 1814, University of Virginia Library Archives, 640/14.

Chapter 4: A Fiery End for the Nancy

153 Drummond to Prevost, 28 January 1814, *Select British Documents of the Canadian War of 1812*, 3 (Part 1):266.

154 For a thorough discussion of the British supply situation during the war, see Glenn A. Steppler, *"A Duty Troublesome Beyond Measure": Logistical Considerations in the Canadian War of 1812* (unpublished MA thesis, 1974).

155 Bullock to Loring, 26 February 1814, *Select British Documents of the Canadian War of 1812*, 3 (Part 1):269.

156 Bullock to Loring, 26 February 1814, *ibid.*, 3 (Part 1):270.

157 Snider, *Leaves from the War Log of the Nancy*, xlii.

158 McDouall is spelled differently in several sources. The modern agreed-upon spelling is McDouall; however, in many printed sources it can be listed as McDowall or McDonall.

159 Winston Johnston, *The Glengarry Light Infantry, 1812-1816* (Charlottetown: Benson Publishing, 1998), 247.

160 Military Secretary to Drummond, 30 January 1814, *The Documentary History of the Campaign on the Niagara Frontier*, 9:155–56.

161 Snider, *Leaves from the War Log of the Nancy*, xxxvii.

162 *Ibid.*, xxxvii-xxxviii.

163 *Ibid.*, xxxviii.

164 *Ibid.*, xxxix.

165 *Ibid.*

166 *Ibid.*, xl.

167 Yeo to Prevost, 8 February 1814, *The Documentary History of the Campaign on the Niagara Frontier*, 9:171.

168 McDouall to Drummond, 26 May 1814, *Select British Documents of the Canadian War of 1812*, 3 (Part 1):272.

169 *Ibid.*

170 McDonall to Drummond, 17 July 1814, *Michigan Pioneer and Historical Society Collection*, 15:617.

171 Sinclair to Secretary of the Navy, 7 April 1814, *The Documentary History of the Campaign on the Niagara Frontier*, 9:283. Sinclair inherited an unwanted command. Following the battle of Lake Erie, the ill Perry was promoted and sent to the east coast. Elliot was left in command at Erie. Afraid that his career would be stifled by an isolated command like Lake Erie, Elliot asked to be relieved of his responsibilities on the lakes. Some of Perry's officers had questioned Elliot's actions during the Battle of Lake Erie, and Elliot sought to protect his reputation by convening a court of inquiry. The inquiry was eventually held in April 1815, but in the meantime Sinclair was left to deal with a command that had suffered from the neglect of its commanding officer. For more details on the Perry-Elliot controversy, see David W. Francis, "Politics, Sectionalism and the Naval Officer Corps: The Perry-Elliot Controversy," in *Inland Seas*, 59, 3 (2003): 200–217.

172 Sinclair to Secretary of the Navy, 29 April 1814, *The Documentary History of the Campaign on the Niagara Frontier*, 9:317.

173 Heads of Plan of Campaign within District No. 9, *ibid.*, 9:321.

174 Croghan to Sinclair, 1 May 1814. *ibid.*, 333.

175 A. Sinclair to J.H. Cooke, 10 May 1814, University of Virginia Library Archives, 640/16.

176 Talbot to Riall, 16 May 1814, *Select British Documents of the Canadian War of 1812*, 3 (Part 1):88.

177 Drummond to Prevost, 27 May 1814, *Select British Documents of the Canadian War of 1812*, 3 (Part 1):91–92.

178 Wesley B. Turner, *British Generals in the War of 1812: High Command in the Canadas* (Montreal: McGill-Queen's University Press, 1999), 113–17.

179   Sinclair to Secretary of the Navy, 19 May 1814, Letters Received by the Secretary of the Navy from Captains, MF463 (M125, Roll no. 36, 81).

180   Stanley, *War of 1812 Land Operations*, 280.

181   George Sheppard, *Plunder, Profit and Paroles: A Social History of the War of 1812 in Upper Canada* (Montreal: McGill-Queen's University Press, 1999), 162.

182   Sinclair to Secretary of the Navy, 27 May 1814, Letters Received by the Secretary of the Navy from Captains, MF463 (M125, Roll no. 36, 106).

183   Yeo to Worsley, 2 July 1814, *Michigan Pioneer and Historical Society Collection*, 15:601.

184   Unknown to W.D. Thomas, 6 August 1814, U.S. National Archives, RG45, CL, 1814, Vol. 6, Enclosure to No. 10 (M125, Roll no. 39).

185   Invoice of provisions and invoice of stores forwarded by Deputy Asst. Commissary General Crookshank to the Post of Michilimackinac, on Board his Majesty's Schooner *Nancy*, signed Miller Worsley, dated 2 August 1814, *Michigan Pioneer and Historical Society Collection*, 15:632.

186   Inhabitants of Prairie du Chien to Roberts, 10 February 1813, *Select British Documents of the Canadian War of 1812*, 3 (Part 1):253.

187   McDouall to Drummond, 16 July 1814, *Select British Documents of the Canadian War of 1812*, 3 (Part 1):254.

188   McKay to McDouall, 27 July 1814, *ibid.*, 3 (Part 1):257.

189   McKay's supplement, 29 July 1814, *ibid.*, 3 (Part 1):264.

190   McKay to McDouall, 27 July 1814, *ibid.*, 3 (Part 1):259.

191   Quimby, *The U.S. Army in the War of 1812*, 2:745.

192   Sinclair to Cooke, 3 September 1814, University of Virginia Library, 640/17.

193   Quimby, *U.S. Army in the War of 1812*, 2:746.

194   *Ibid.*, 746.

195   McDouall to Prevost, 14 August 1814, *Select British Documents of the Canadian War of 1812*, 3 (Part 1):274.

196   McDouall to Prevost, 14 August 1814, *Select British Documents of the Canadian War of 1812*, 3 (Part 1):275.

197   Quimby, *U.S. Army in the War of 1812*, 2:747.

198 See Livingston's petition to Drummond and Earl of Dalhousie, 1815, in *The Documentary History of the Campaign on the Niagara Frontier*, 7:37–43.

199 Unknown to W.D. Thomas, 6 August 1814, U.S. National Archives, RG45, CL, 1814, Vol. 6, Enclosure to No. 10 (M125, Roll no. 39).

200 McDowall to Worsley, 28 July 1814, U.S. National Archives, RG45, CL 1814, Vol 6, Enclosure to No. 10 (M125, Roll No. 39).

201 McDouall to Drummond, 28 July 1814, *Michigan Pioneer and Historical Society Collection*, 15:629.

202 Drummond to Prevost, 11 August 1814, *ibid.*, 15:634.

203 Cruikshank, "An Episode of the War of 1812," 149.

204 Quimby, *The U.S. Army in the War of 1812*, 2:748.

205 Worsley to his father, 6 October 1814, in Snider, *Leaves from the War Log of the Nancy*, xlvii.

206 Sinclair to Secretary of the Navy Jones, 3 September 1813, U.S. National Archives, RG 45, CL, 1814, Roll 6, No. 10 (M125, Roll no. 39).

207 A. Sinclair to J.H. Cooke, 3 September 1814, University of Virginia Library Archives, 640/17.

208 Sinclair to Daniel Turner, 15 August 1814. U.S. National Archives, RG 45, CL, 1814, Vol. 5, No. 102. (M125, Roll no. 38)

Chapter 5: Worsley's War

209 Sinclair to Secretary of the Navy Jones, 3 September 1813, U.S. National Archives, RG 45, CL, 1814, Roll 6, No. 10 (M125, Roll no. 39).

210 Elsie McLeod Jury, "*USS Tigress – HMS Confiance*, 1813–1831," *Inland Seas*, 28 (1964): 8.

211 Worsley to his father, October 6, 1814, in Snider, *Leaves from the War Log of the Nancy*, xlvii-xlviii.

212 Enclosed in Crookshank to Turquand, 21 August 1814, *Michigan Pioneer and Historical Society Collection*, 15:637.

213 Worsley to his father, 6 October 1814, in Snider, *Leaves from the War Log of the Nancy*, xlvii-xlviii.

214 Sinclair to Secretary of the Navy Jones, October 28, 1814, U.S. National Archives, RG 45, CL, 1814, Vol. 7, No. 71.

215 Worsley to his father, 6 October 1814, in Snider, *Leaves from the War Log of the Nancy,* xlvii-xlviii.

216 McDouall to Drummond, 9 September 1814, *Michigan Pioneer and Historical Society Collection*, 15:643.

217 Worsley to Yeo, 15 September 1814, Adm.1/2738.

218 George F. Stanley, "British Operations in the American North-West, 1812–1815," *Journal of the Society of Army Historical Research*, 22, no. 87 (Autumn 1943): 99–100.

219 Cruikshank, "An Episode of the War of 1812," 152.

220 Worsley to Yeo, 15 September 1814, Adm.1/2738

221 *Ibid.*

222 McDouall to Drummond, 9 September 1814, *Michigan Pioneer and Historical Society Collection*, 15:643.

223 The invoices for canoes, which left Lachine on 10 September 1814 and 22 September 1814, are found in McDouall to Drummond, 9 September 1814, *Michigan Pioneer and Historical Society Collection*, 15:647–48.

224 Instructions for the distribution of Indian Presents, n.d., signed Sheaffe, *Ibid.*, 15:649.

225 John Askin, Invoice of sundry Indian stores delivered to Robert Dickson Esqr., 29 October 1814, *Ibid.*, 15:656.

226 Sinclair to Secretary of the Navy Jones, 28 October 1814, U.S. National Archives, RG 45, CL, 1814, Vol. 7 No. 71.

227 Cruikshank, "An Episode of the War of 1812," 153.

228 Proceedings of Board of Claims, 14 December 1814, *Michigan Pioneer and Historical Society Collection*, 15:682–84.

229 Hitsman, *The Incredible War of 1812*, 261.

230 Stagg, *Mr. Madison's War*, 471.

231 Yeo to Prevost, 25 February 1815, *Michigan Pioneer and Historical Society Collection*, 16:54–55.

232 Worsley to King William IV, 13 April 1831, reprinted in Gough, *Fighting Sail*, 175–76.

233 McGillivray to Prevost, 28 March 1815, *Select British Documents of the Canadian War of 1812*, 3 (Part 1):527.

234 McDouall to Forster, 15 May 1815, *ibid.*, 534.

CHAPTER 6: FINDING THE BONES OF THE NANCY: C.H.J. SNIDER

235 For more information on the role of the Nottawasaga, and especially Penetanguishene, in the aftermath of the War of 1812, see Gough, *Fighting Sail*, chapters 7, 8 and 9.

236 C.H.J. Snider, "From a Stick to a Ship — the '*Nancy*'s' Figurehead," *Toronto Evening Telegram*, December 23, 1933, 8.

237 Invoices of stores and provisions forwarded to Michilimackinac, endorsed Miller Worsley 2 August 1814, *Michigan Pioneer and Historical Society Collection*, 15:632.

238 Robert B. Townsend, ed., *Tales from the Great Lakes: Based on C.H.J. Snider's "Schooner Days"* (Toronto: Dundurn, 1995), 17–19.

239 C.H.J. Snider, *The Story of the "Nancy" and other Eighteen-Twelvers* (Toronto: McClelland and Stewart, 1927), 63–64.

240 Modern hydrography has determined that very low water levels in the lakes in the early twentieth century were linked to larger meteorological phenomenon, like the great western dust bowl of the 1930s. Lake levels fluctuate wildly and unpredictably under natural circumstances. See *Living with the Lakes* (U.S. Army Corps of Engineers and Great Lakes Commission, 1999), 17.

241 Snider, *The Story of the "Nancy" and other Eighteen-Twelvers*, 65–66.

242 *Ibid.*, 66.

243 *Ibid.*, 67-68.

244 *Ibid.*, 68; Chris Skeaff and Michael Gurr, *HMS Nancy* (Wasaga Beach, Ont.: Friends of Nancy Island / Wasaga Beach Provincial Park, 2002), 11–12.

245 Thor A. Conway, "Archeological Fieldwork at the Schoonertown Naval Establishment on Lake Huron," *Canadian Archeological Association Collected Papers*, Research Report 6 (Government of Ontario: Historic Sites Branch, Division of Parks, March 1975), 9.

246 *Wasaga Beach Provincial Park Preliminary Master Plan* (Ontario Ministry of Natural Resources, September 1974), 12.

Postscript

247 R. Alan Douglas, *Uppermost Canada: the Western District and the Detroit Frontier, 1800–1850* (Detroit: Wayne State University Press, 2001), 94–95.
248 Lajeunesse, *The Windsor Border Region*, 200.
249 Skeaff and Gurr, *HMS Nancy*, 6.
250 Marshall, *Royal Naval Biography (London, 1831)*, 4 (Part 1):374.
251 Antal, *A Wampum Denied*, 393.
252 Johnston, *The Glengarry Light Infantry, 1812–1816*, 248.
253 Norma Lois Peterson, *The Presidencies of William Henry Harrison and John Tyler* (Lawrence, Kans.: University Press of Kansas, 1989), 18–19.

Selected Bibliography

MANUSCRIPTS

ARCHIVES OF ONTARIO, TORONTO, ONTARIO:

Hiram Walker Historical Museum Collection, MU 10309 (micro-
form copies of originals at Windsor Historical Museum,
Windsor, Ontario)

NATIONAL ARCHIVES OF CANADA, OTTAWA, ONTARIO:

Colonial Office Papers, copies of C.O.42 series; also assorted C.series
documents of the War Department and Officers Commanding on
the defence of Upper Canada.

THE NATIONAL ARCHIVES, KEW, SURREY:

Adm.1. Various volumes on the Great Lakes, and in particular the papers
of the Commodore and Commandant at Kingston, Upper Canada;
also various in-letters from commanders of vessels. Of special
interest: Adm.1/503, Admiral Sir John Warren's correspondence
with Captain Robert Heriot Barclay; Adm.1/2737, Barclay's narrative given at his court martial, 9 September 1814; and Adm.1/5445
(Court Martial documents); also, Adm.1/2736, Commodore Sir

James Lucas Yeo's report to Admiral Warren on loss of H.M. Fleet on Lake Erie; also, Adm.1/2738, Miller Worsley's report of proceedings, capture of *Tigress* and *Scorpion*, U.S.N. schooners, 1814.

Adm.9. Service record of Robert Heriot Barclay (v.4, no.1241); service record of Miller Worsley (v.5, no.1571).

Adm.12/193. Digest of correspondence, 1819.

Adm.49/10. Prize papers relative to taking of U.S.N. schooners *Tigress* and *Scorpion*, complete to closing of file in 1820.

Adm.106/1998, 1999 and 2002. Statements of naval force.

UNITED STATES NATIONAL ARCHIVES:

RG21. Prize case files for the U.S. District Court for the Eastern District of Pennsylvania, being cases of North West Company's *Mink* and *Perseverance* (copies are in Naval Historical Center, microfilm M966, roll 2).

RG45, CL, 1814, v.3 and 4. Crogan-Sinclair correspondence 1814. Also, v.5 and 6, Jones- Sinclair and Turner-Sinclair correspondence 1814.

RG125, v.6, no.207. Court of inquiry into conduct of Stephen Champlin in the loss of *Tigress* and Daniel Turner in the loss of *Scorpion*, 1814 (microfilm copy in Naval Historical Center, Washington D.C., M273, roll 7).

PRINTED DOCUMENTS

Cruikshank, Edward A., ed. *The Documentary History of the Campaign upon the Niagara Frontier*. 9 vols. Welland, Ont.: Tribune Office for the Lundy's Lane Historical Society, 1902–1908.

———. *Documents Relating to the Invasion of Canada and the Surrender of Detroit, 1812.* Ottawa: Canadian Archives Publications, no. 7, Government Printing Bureau, 1912.

Dudley, William, and Crawford, Michael, eds. *The Naval War of 1812: A Documentary History.* 3 vols. Washington: Naval Historical Center, 1985, 1992, 2003.

Lajeunesse, Ernest J., ed. *The Windsor Border Region: Canada's Southernmost Frontier, A Collection of Documents.* Toronto: Champlain Society, 1960.

Leaves from the War Log of the Nancy, *Eighteen Hundred and Thirteen, with Comments by C.H.J. Snider.* New ed. Midland, Ont.: Huronia Historical Development Council, 1968.

Michigan Pioneer and Historical Society Collection. Vol. 15, Lansing, Mich.: Robert Smith Printing Co., 1889.

Quaife, Milo M., ed. *John Askin Papers.* 2 vols. Detroit: Detroit Library Commission, 1928.

Wallace, W. Stewart, ed. *Documents Relating to the North West Company.* Toronto: Champlain Society, 1934.

Wood, William, ed. *Select British Documents of the Canadian War of 1812.* 3 vols. Toronto: Champlain Society, 1920–1928.

SECONDARY WORKS

Antal, Sandy. *A Wampum Denied: Procter's War of 1812.* Ottawa: Carleton University Press, 1997.

Berton, Pierre. *The Invasion of Canada, 1812–1813.* Toronto: McClelland and Stewart, 1980.

———. *Flames Across the Border, 1813–1814*. Toronto: McClelland and Stewart, 1981.

Cruikshank, Edward A. "An Episode of the War of 1812: The Story of the Schooner *Nancy* [with illustrative documents]," *Ontario Historical Society Papers and Records*, 9 (1910), reprinted in Morris Zaslow, ed., *The Defended Border: Upper Canada and the War of 1812*. Toronto: Macmillan of Canada, 1964.

Douglas, R. Alan. *Uppermost Canada: the Western District and the Detroit Frontier, 1800–1850*. Detroit: Wayne State University Press, 2001.

Douglas, W.A.B. "Worsley, Miller." *Dictionary of Canadian Biography*. Vol. 6. Toronto: University of Toronto Press, 1986.

Francis, David F. "Politics, Sectionalism and the Naval Officer Corps: The Perry-Elliot Controversy." *Inland Seas* 59, 2003.

Garraty, John A. and Mark Carnes, eds. *Dictionary of American National Biography*. New York: Oxford University Press, 1999.

Gilpin, Alec R. *The War of 1812 in the Old Northwest*. East Lansing, Mich.: Michigan State University Press, 1958.

Gough, Barry. *Fighting Sail on Lake Huron and Georgian Bay: The War of 1812 and its Aftermath*. Annapolis, Md.: Naval Institute Press, St. Catharines, Ontario: Vanwell Publishing, 2002.

Gray, William. *Soldiers of the King: The Upper Canada Militia 1812-1815, A Reference Guide*. Erin, Ont.: Boston Mills Press, 1995.

Hickey, Donald R. *The War of 1812: A Forgotten Conflict*. Urbana, Ill.: University of Illinois Press, 1989.

Hagan, Kenneth, ed. *In Peace and War: Interpretations of American Naval History, 1775–1984*. Westport, Conn.: Greenwood, 1984.

Hitsman, J. Mackay. *The Incredible War of 1812: A Military History.* New edition. Toronto: Robin Brass, 1999.

Horsman, Reginald. *The War of 1812.* New York: Alfred A. Knopf, 1969.

Johnston, Winston. *The Glengarry Light Infantry, 1812–1816.* Charlottetown: Benson Publishing, 1998.

Lossing, Benson J. *The Pictorial Field-Book of the War of 1812.* New York: Harper, 1869.

Lucas, Charles P. *The Canadian War of 1812.* Oxford: Clarendon Press, 1906.

McAfee, Robert B. *History of the Late War in the Western Country.* Bowling Green, O.: Historical Publications, 1919. (Originally published 1816.)

Mackenzie, Robert Holden. *The Trafalgar Roll: Containing the Names and Services of all Officers of the Royal Navy and Royal Marines who Participated in the Glorious Victory of the 21st October 1805, together with a History of the Ships Engaged in the Battle.* London: George Allen, 1913.

Jury, Elsie McLeod. "*USS Tigress – HMS Confiance,* 1813–1831." *Inland Seas* 28 (1964), 3–16.

Mahan, Alfred.T. *Sea Power in its Relations to the War of 1812.* 2 vols. Boston: Little, Brown, 1905.

Malcomson, Robert. *Lords of the Lake: The Naval War on Lake Ontario, 1812-1814.* Toronto: Robin Bass Studio, 1998.

———. "War on the Lakes: The Struggle on the Inland Sea, 1812–1814." *The Beaver* 70, April–May 1990, 44–52.

Marshall, John. *Royal Naval Biography.* London: Longman, Reese, Orme, Brown and Green, 1831.

Ontario. Ministry of Natural Resources. *HMS Nancy and the War of 1812*. New edition. Toronto: Government of Ontario Publications, 1978.

Nicholson, G.W.L. *The Fighting Newfoundlander*. n.p.: Government of Newfoundland, 1964.

Peterson, Norma Lois. *The Presidencies of William Henry Harrison and John Tyler*. Lawrence, Kans.: University Press of Kansas, 1989.

Pryke, K.G., and L.L. Kulisek, eds. *The Western District: Papers from the Western District Conference*. Windsor: Essex County Historical Society, 1983.

Quimby, Robert S. *The U.S. Army in the War of 1812: An Operational and Command Study*. 2 vols. East Lansing, Mich.: Michigan State University Press, 1997.

Richardson, John. *Richardson's War of 1812, with Notes and a Life of the Author by Alexander Clark Casselman*. Toronto: Coles, 1974.

Roosevelt, Theodore. *The Naval War of 1812, or the History of the United States Navy during the Last War with Great Britain to Which is Appended an Account of the Battle of New Orleans*. Annapolis, Md.: Naval Institute Press, 1987. Originally published 1907 by Putnam.

Rosenberg, Max. *The Building of Perry's Fleet on Lake Erie 1812-1813*. Harrisburg, Pa.: Pennsylvania Historical and Museum Commission, 1997.

Skaggs, David Curtis, and Gerard T. Altoff. *A Signal Victory: The Lake Erie Campaign 1812–1813*. Annapolis, Md.: Naval Institute Press, 1997.

Skeaff, Chris, and Michael Gurr. *HMS Nancy*. Wasaga Beach, Ont.: Friends of Nancy Island and Wasaga Beach Provincial Park, 2002.

Snider, C.H.J. *In the Wake of the Eighteen-Twelvers: Fights & Flights of Frigates & Fore-'n'-Afters in the War of 1812–1815 on the Great Lakes.* Toronto: Bell & Cockburn, 1913.

———. *The Story of the "Nancy" and other Eighteen-Twelvers.* Toronto: McClelland & Stewart, 1926.

Stagg, J.C.A. *Mr. Madison's War: Politics, Diplomacy and Warfare in the Early American Republic, 1783–1830.* Princeton, N.J.: Princeton University Press, 1983.

Stanley, George F.G. "British Operations in the American North-West, 1812–1815." *Journal of the Society of Army Historical Research* 22, Autumn 1943.

———. *The War of 1812: Land Operations.* Toronto: Macmillan, 1983.

Turner, Wesley B. *British Generals in the War of 1812: High Command in the Canadas.* Montreal: McGill-Queen's University Press, 1999.

Zaslow, Morris, ed. *The Defended Border.* Toronto: Macmillan, 1964.

Index